Camera Stochastikós

pedestrian images

David Diethelm

Aurora Books, an imprint of Eco-Justice Press, L.L.C.

Aurora Books
P.O. Box 5409 Eugene, OR 97405
www.ecojusticepress.com

Camera Stochastikós: pedestrian images
by David Diethelm

Cover image 'Shadows and dust' by David Diethelm

Library of Congress Control Number: 2020931158
ISBN: 978-1-945432-35-4

About the book:

The photos in this book were taken from a pedestiran perspective - unusual things relating to road construction, amusing markings sprayed on the road, intriguing wrapped fire hydrants - a fashion show of sorts. The 'shaming' of various equipment is totally unintended, but when anthropomorphizing, it becomes hilarious.
Most of the remaining images are just interesting patterns seen while walking around the neighborhood.

The "Stochastikós" in the title is the Greek origin of the English "stochastic". Since the photos are quite random, it seemed right.

* Please excuse the bad puns.

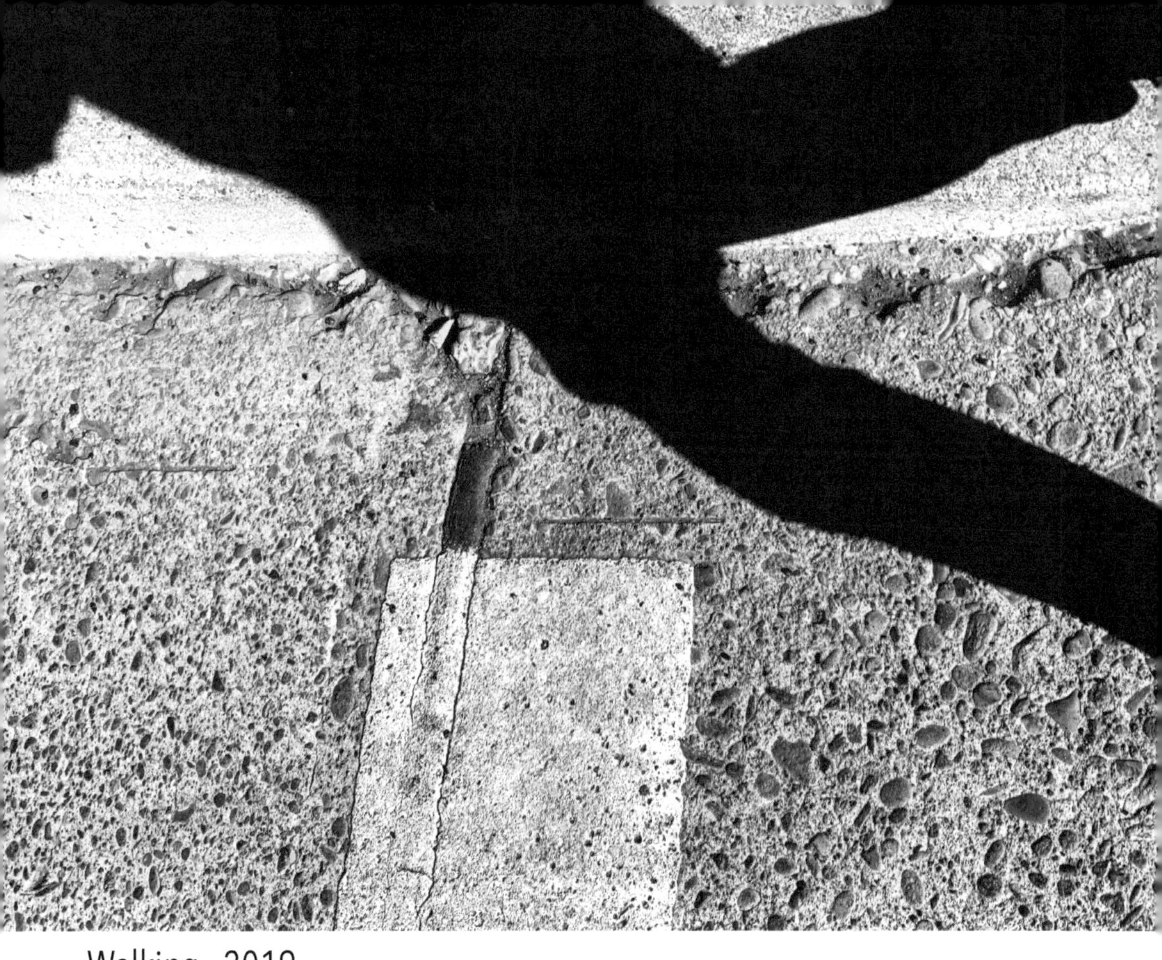

Walking - 2019

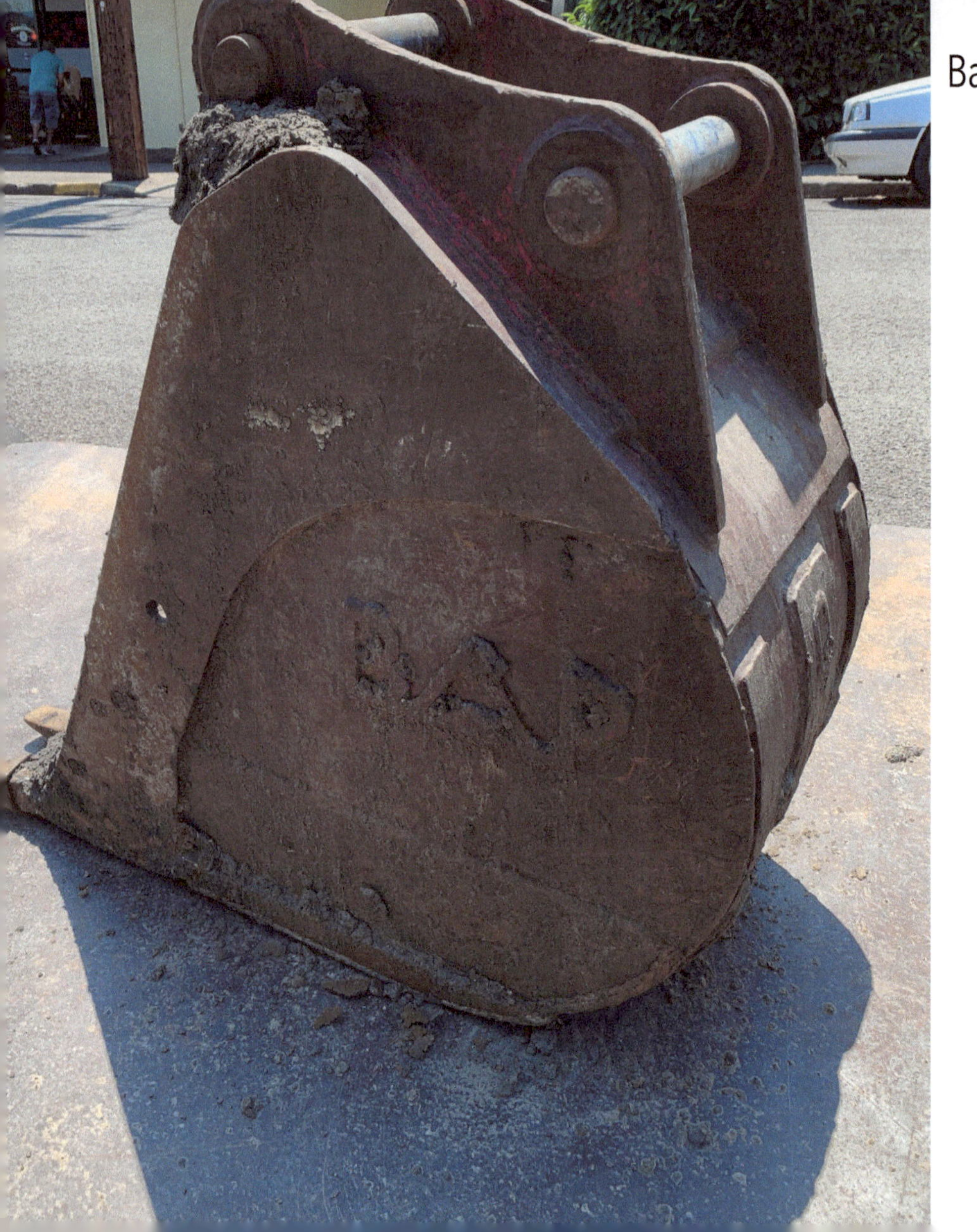

Bad - 2019

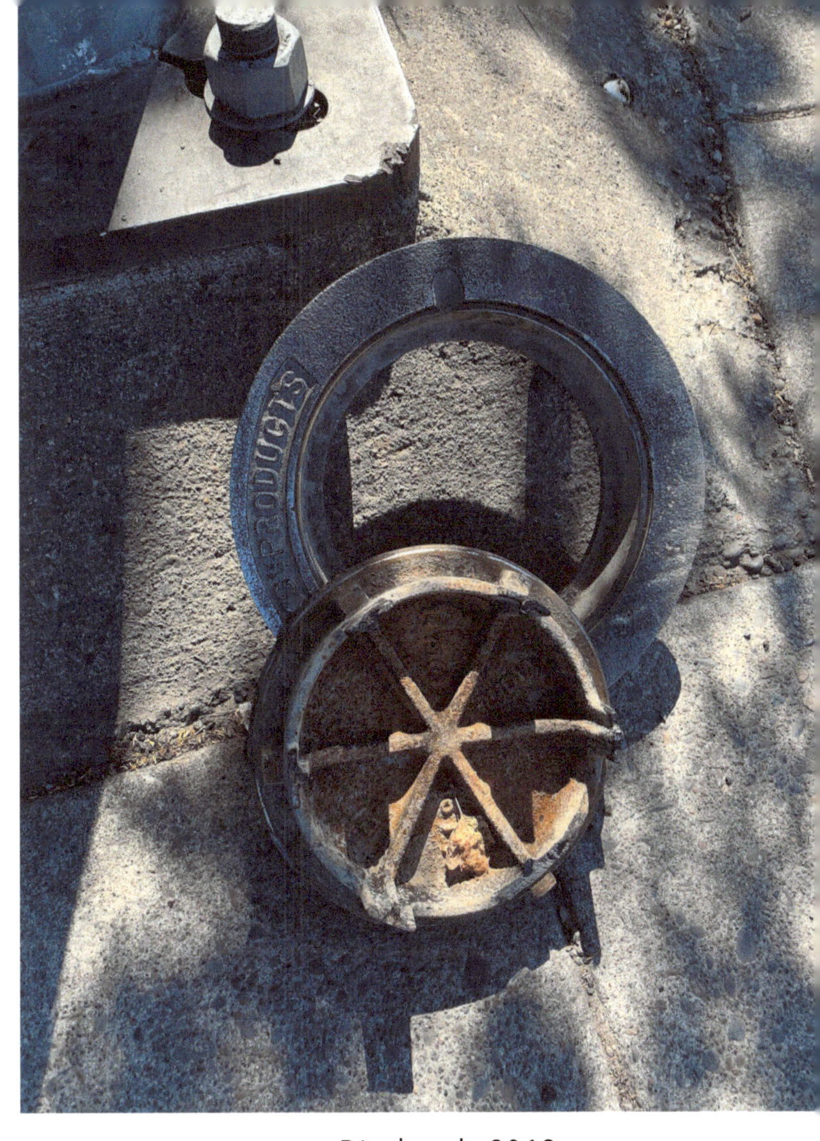

Displaced - 2019

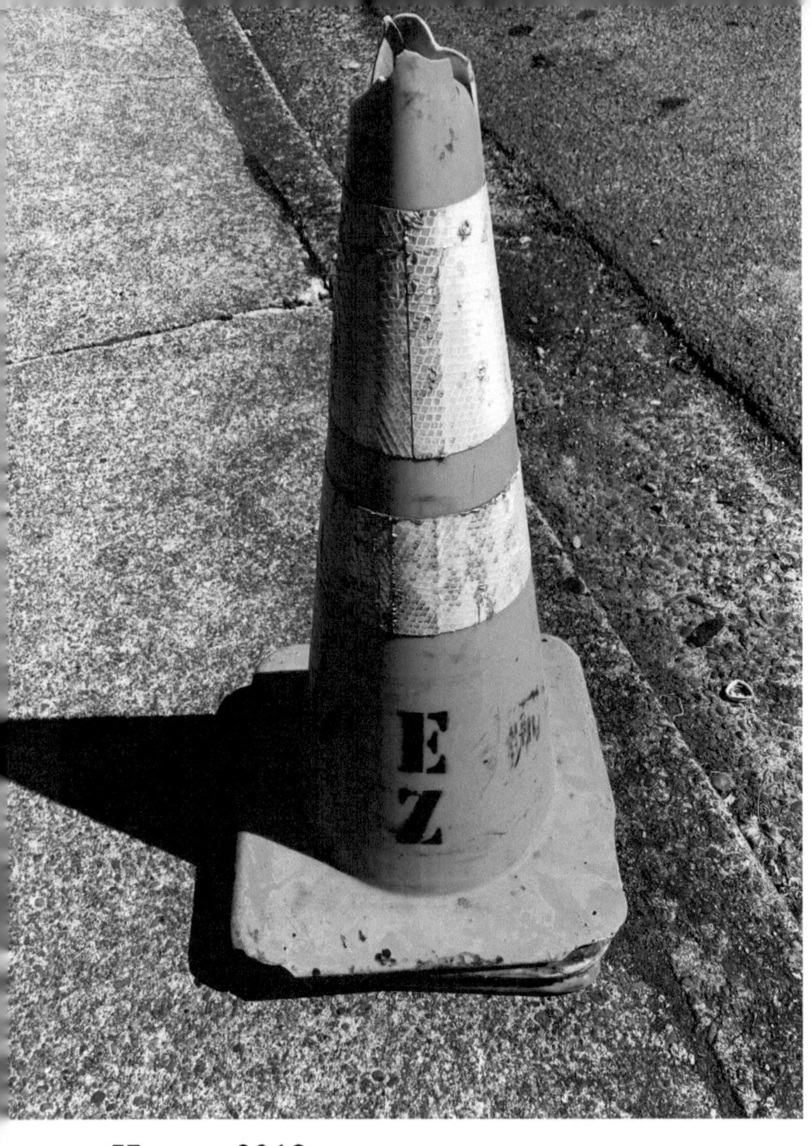

EZ cone - 2019

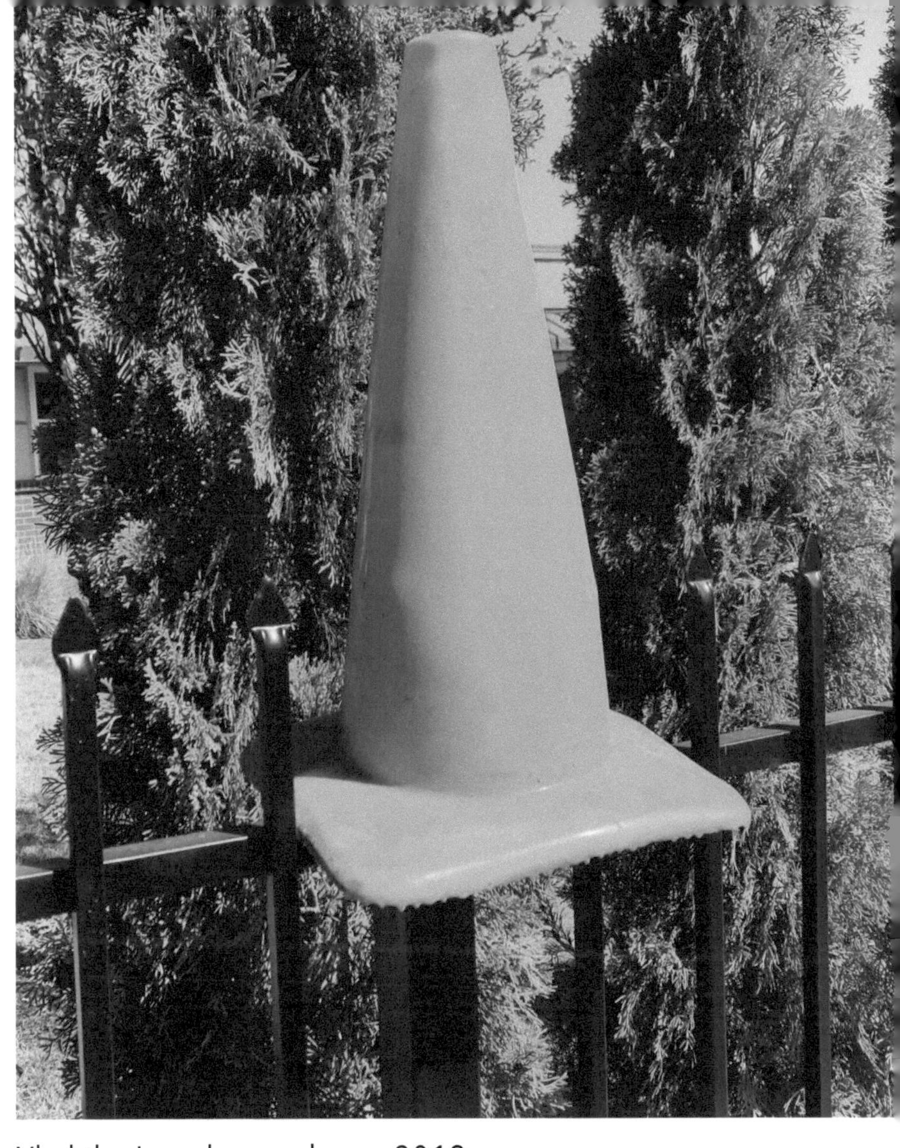

Vlad the Impaler was here - 2019

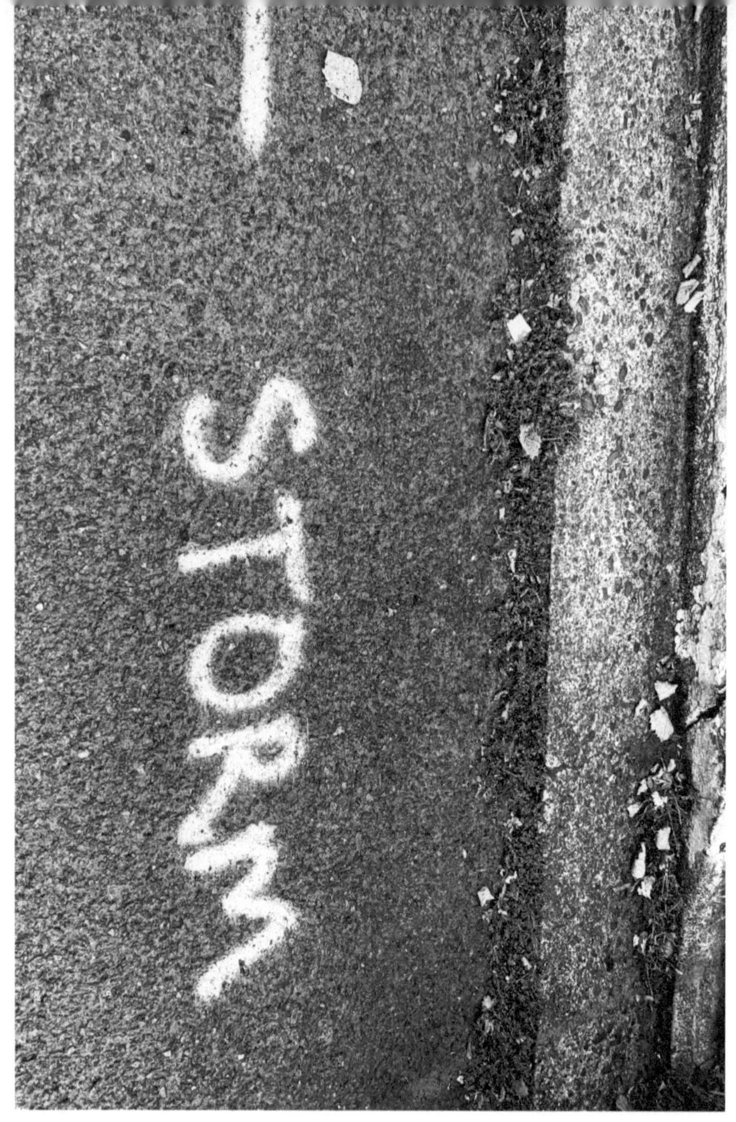

Accurate - 2019

The red Hunt's for October - 2019

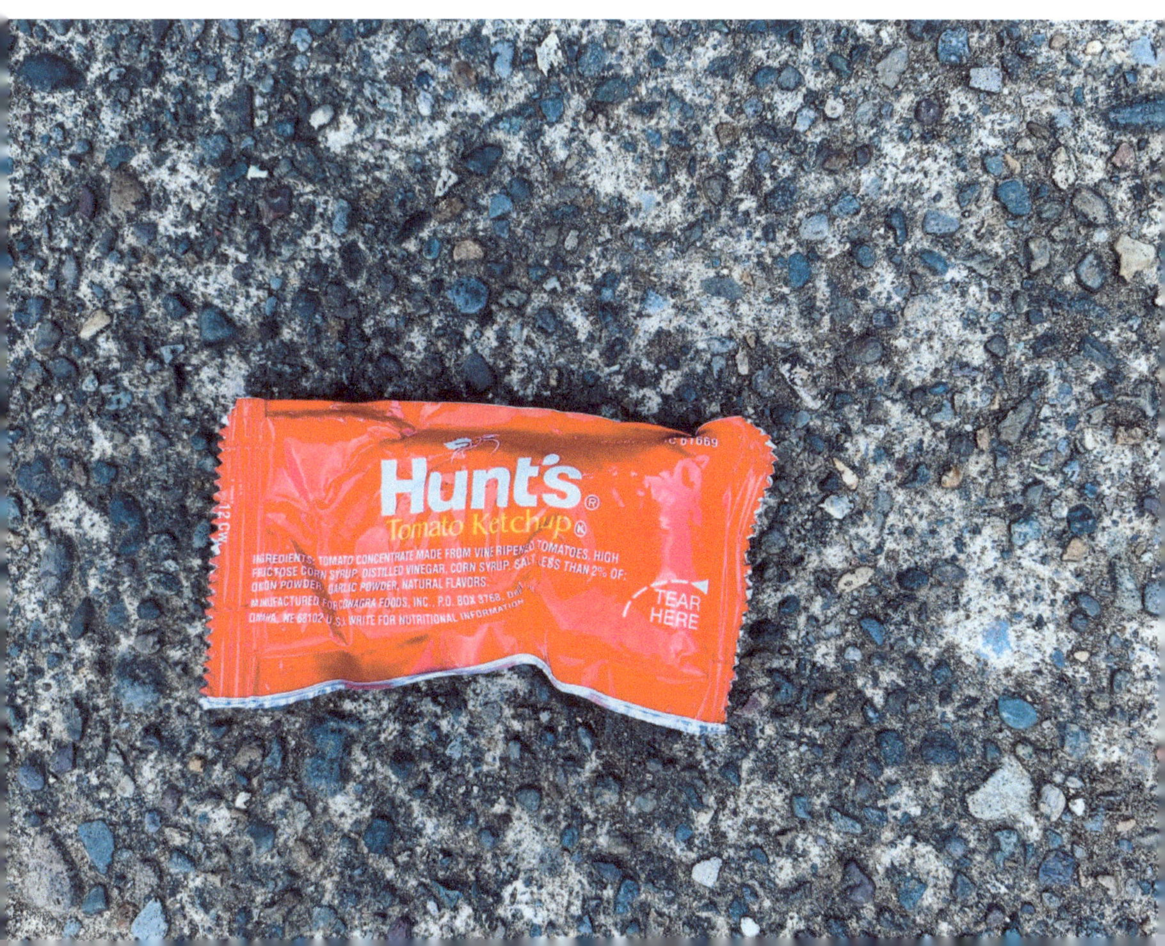

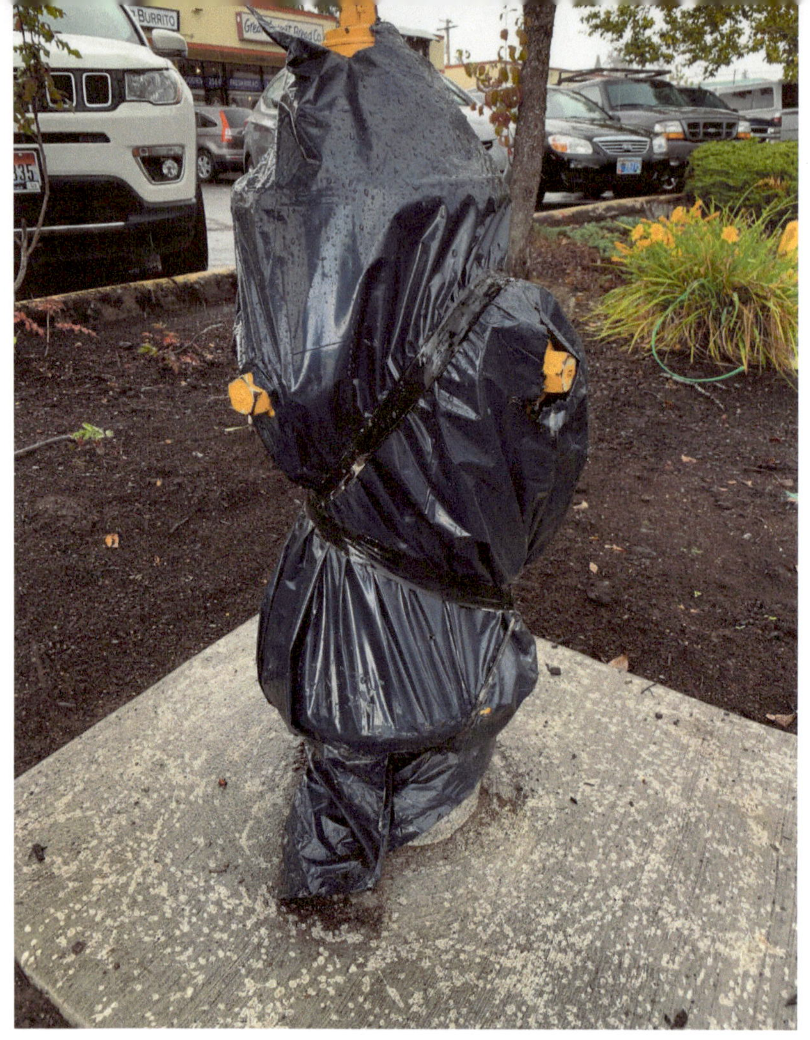

Fire hydrant fashion #1 - 2019

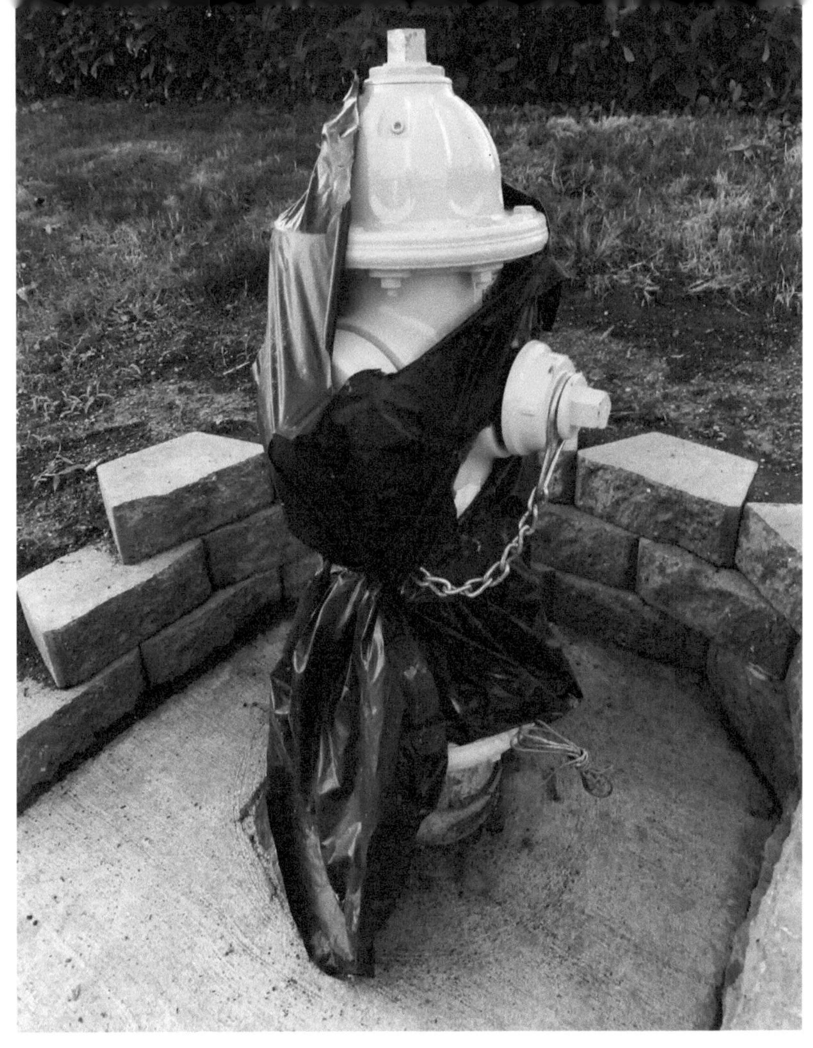

Fire hydrant fashion #2 - 2019

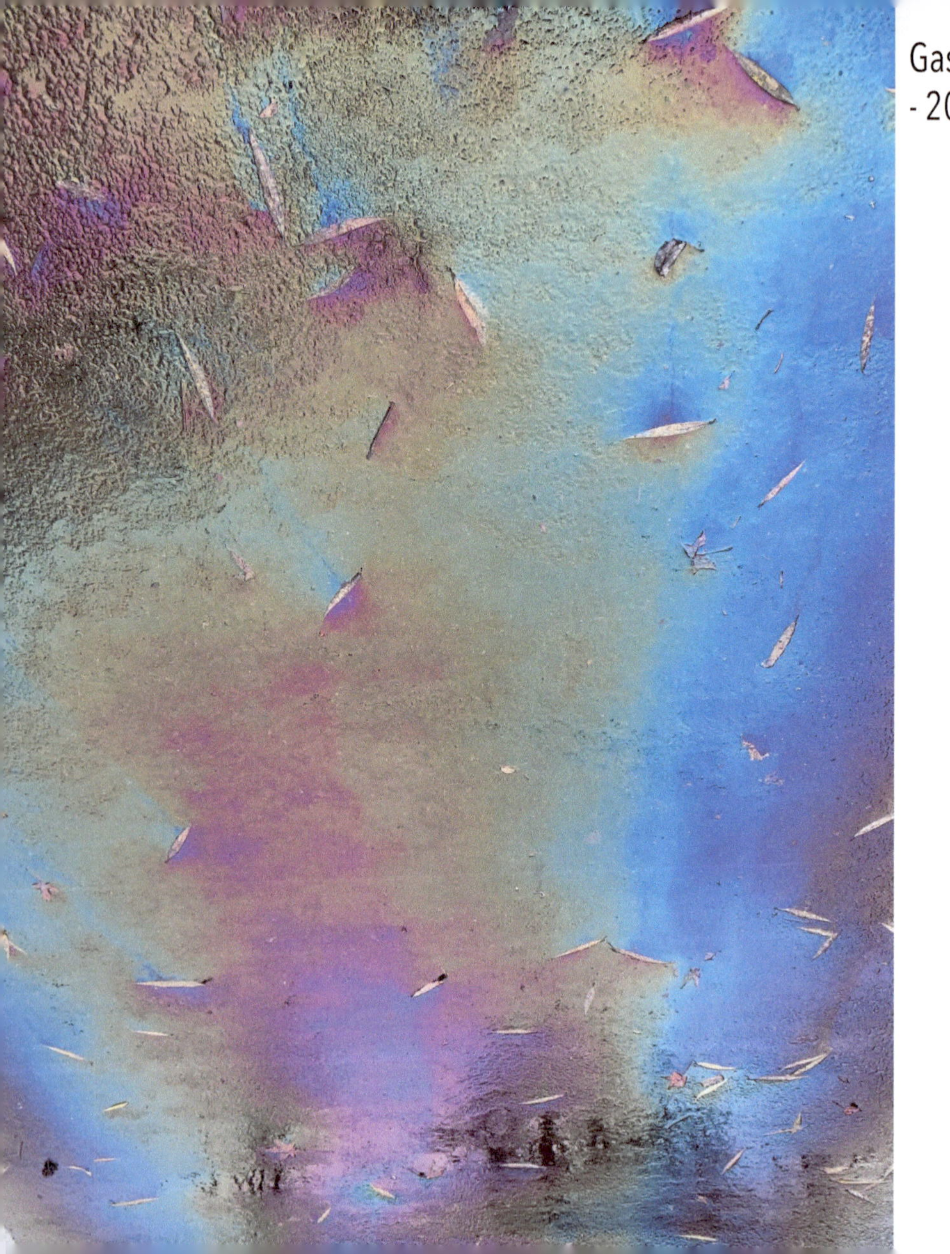

Gasoline aurora
- 2019

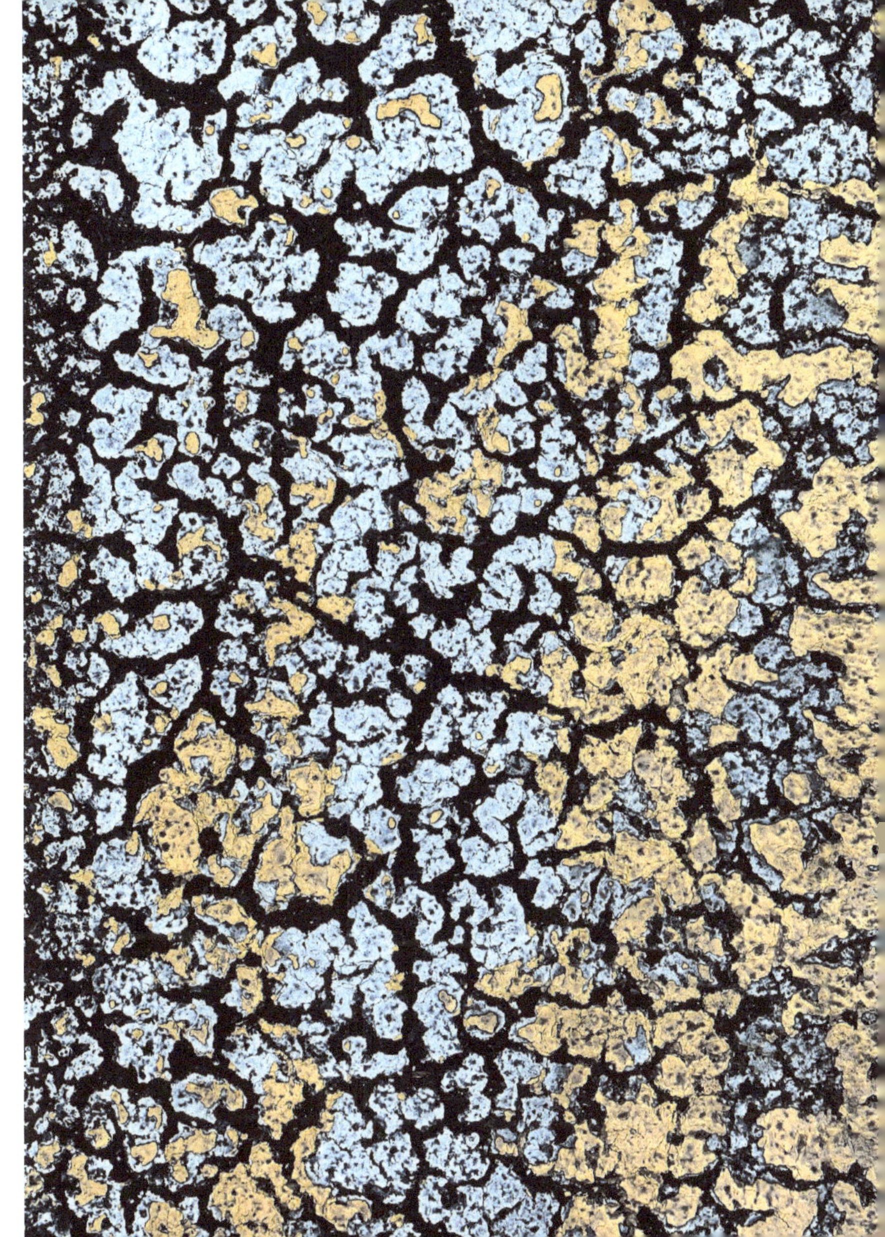

Paint lichen
- 2019

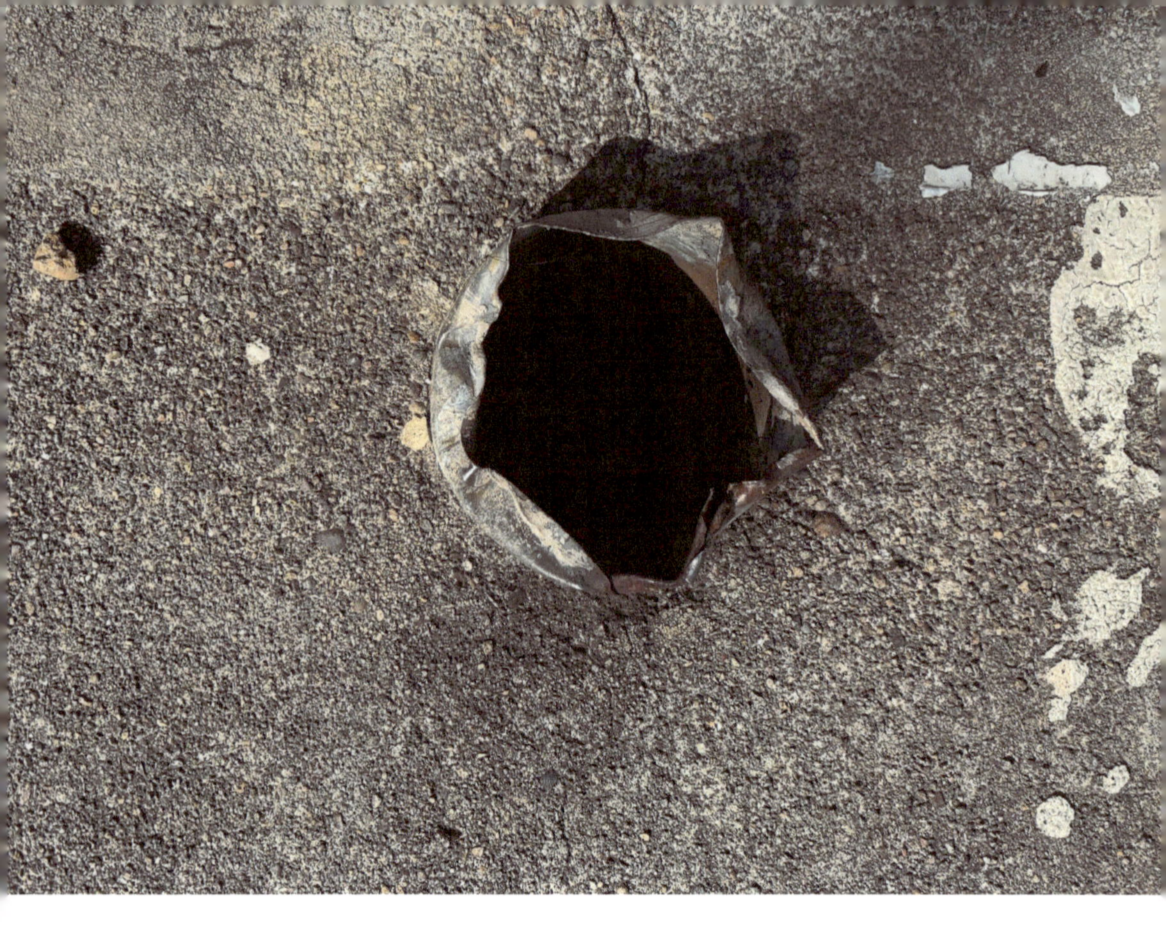

Small black hole - 2019

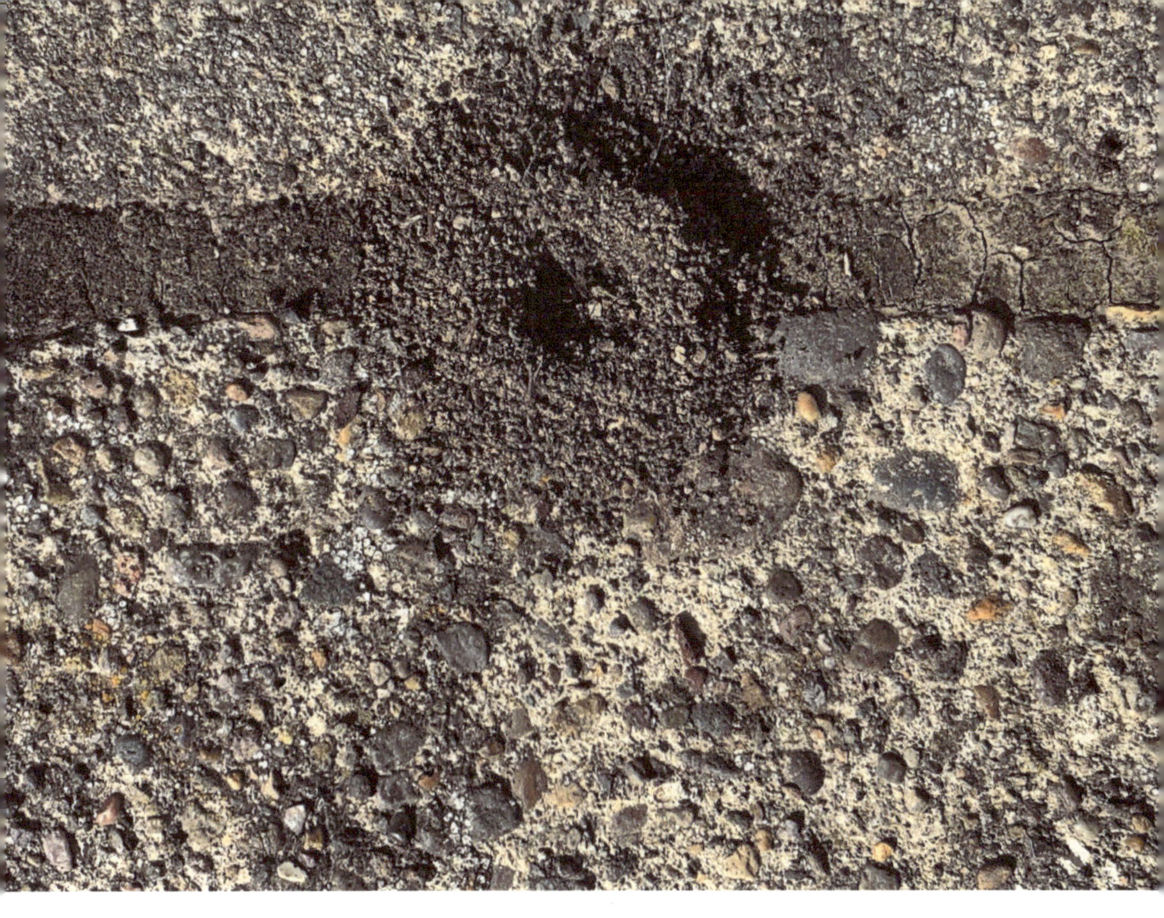

Ant architecture project - 2019

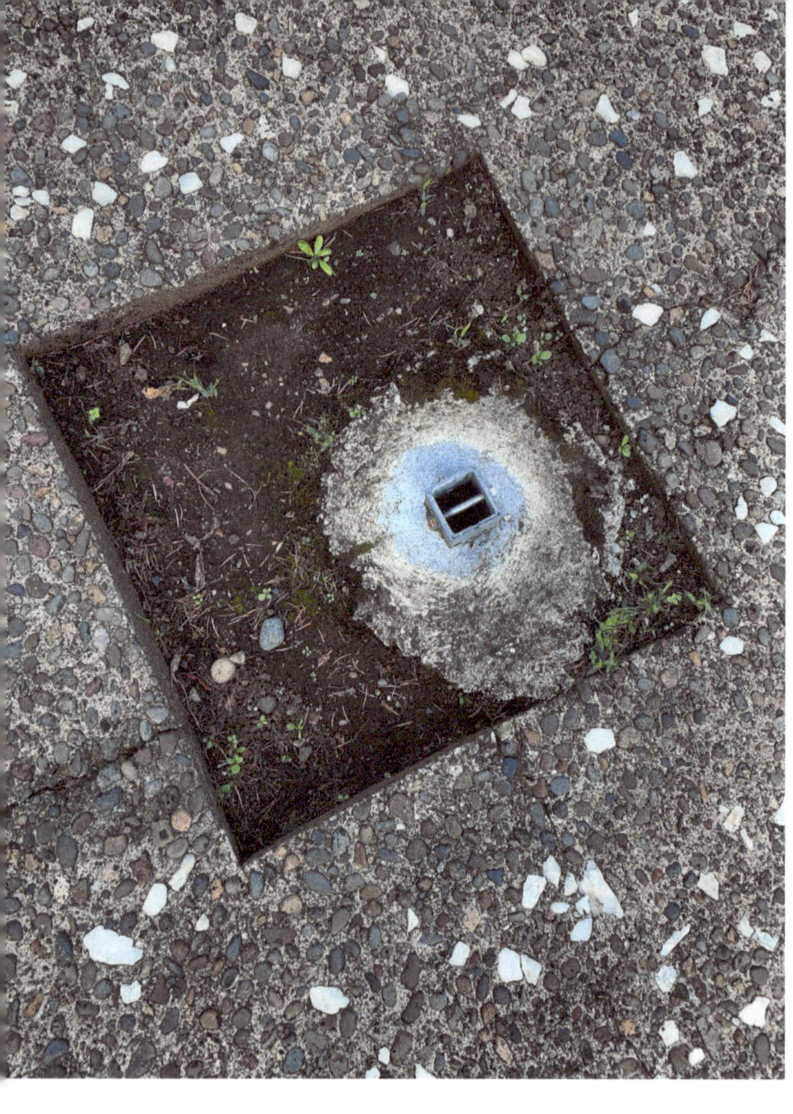

Bus stop has
stopped - 2019

Food remembered,
list, not - 2019

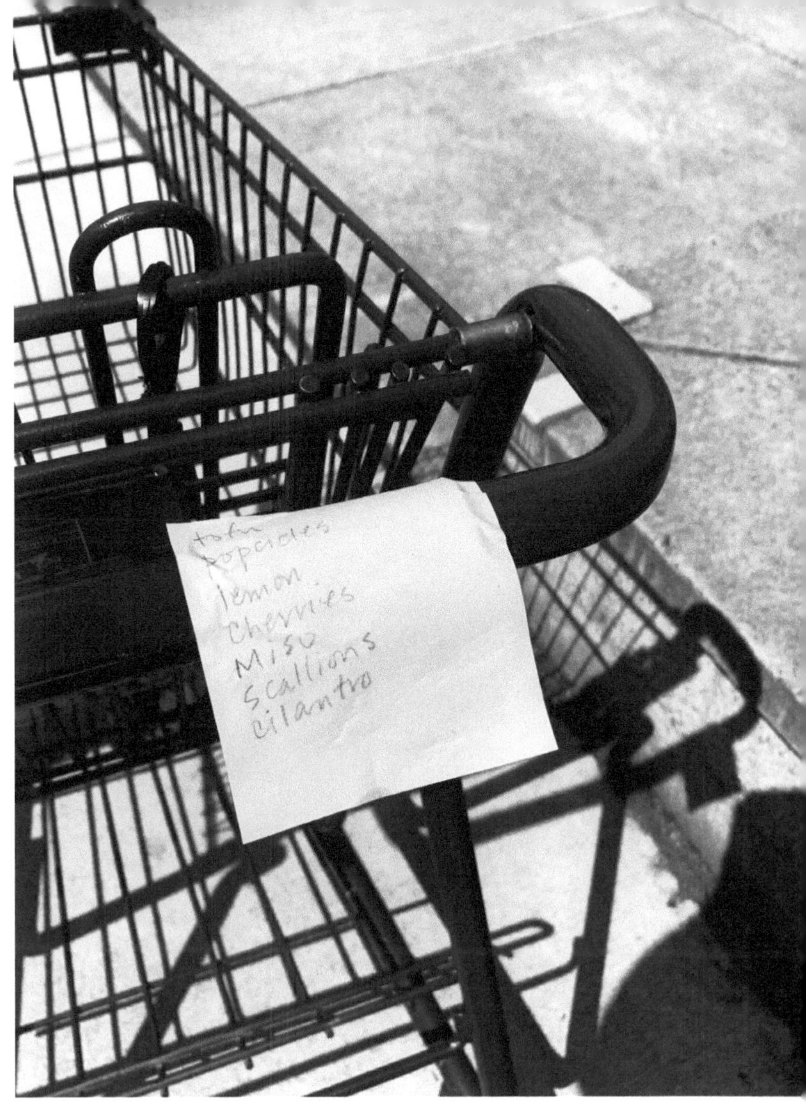

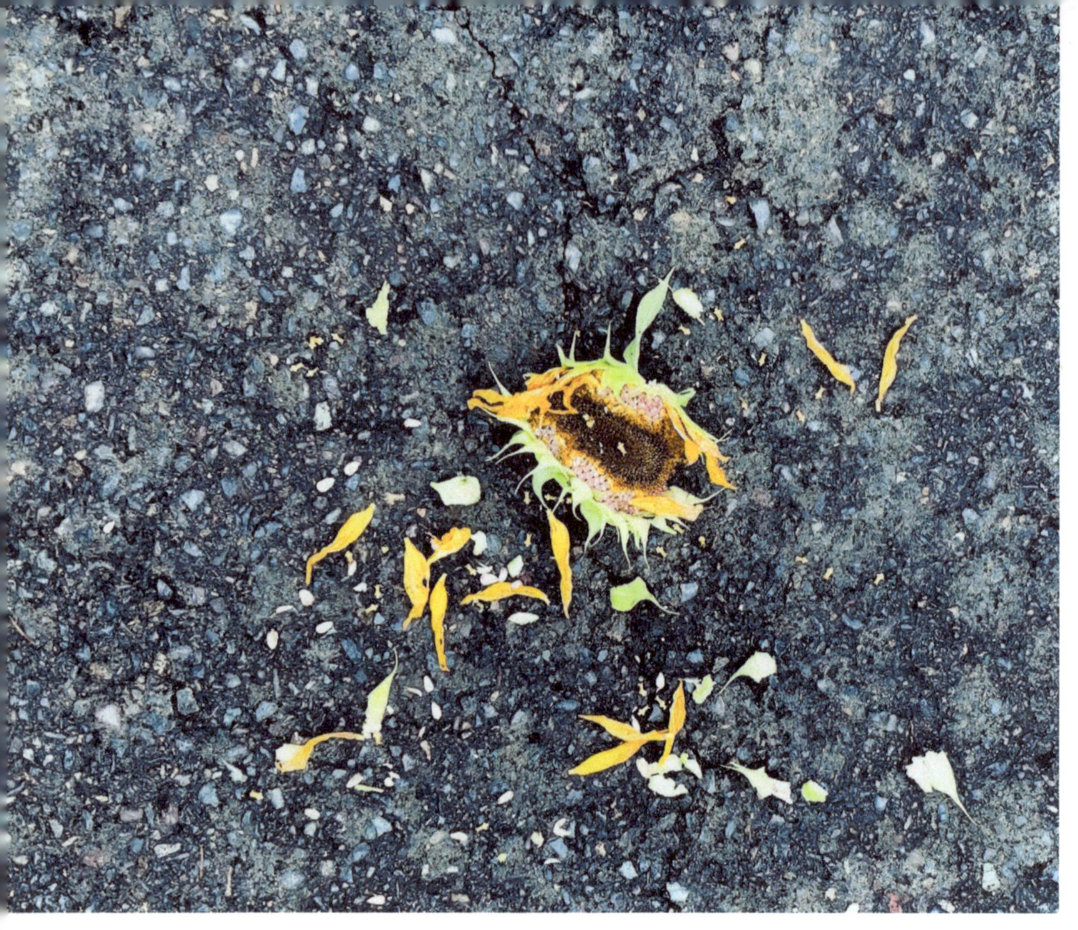

Sun(flower) gone supernova - 2019

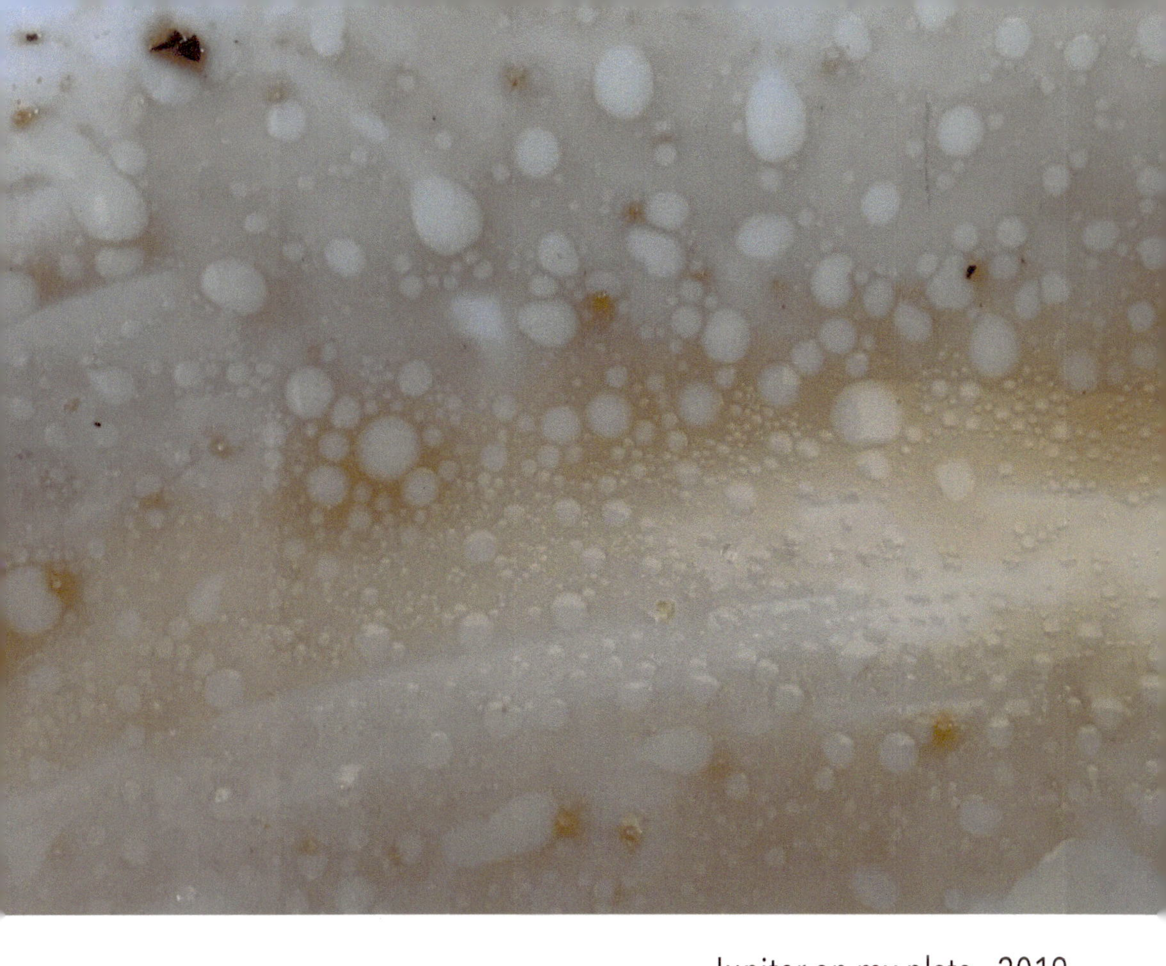

Jupiter on my plate - 2019

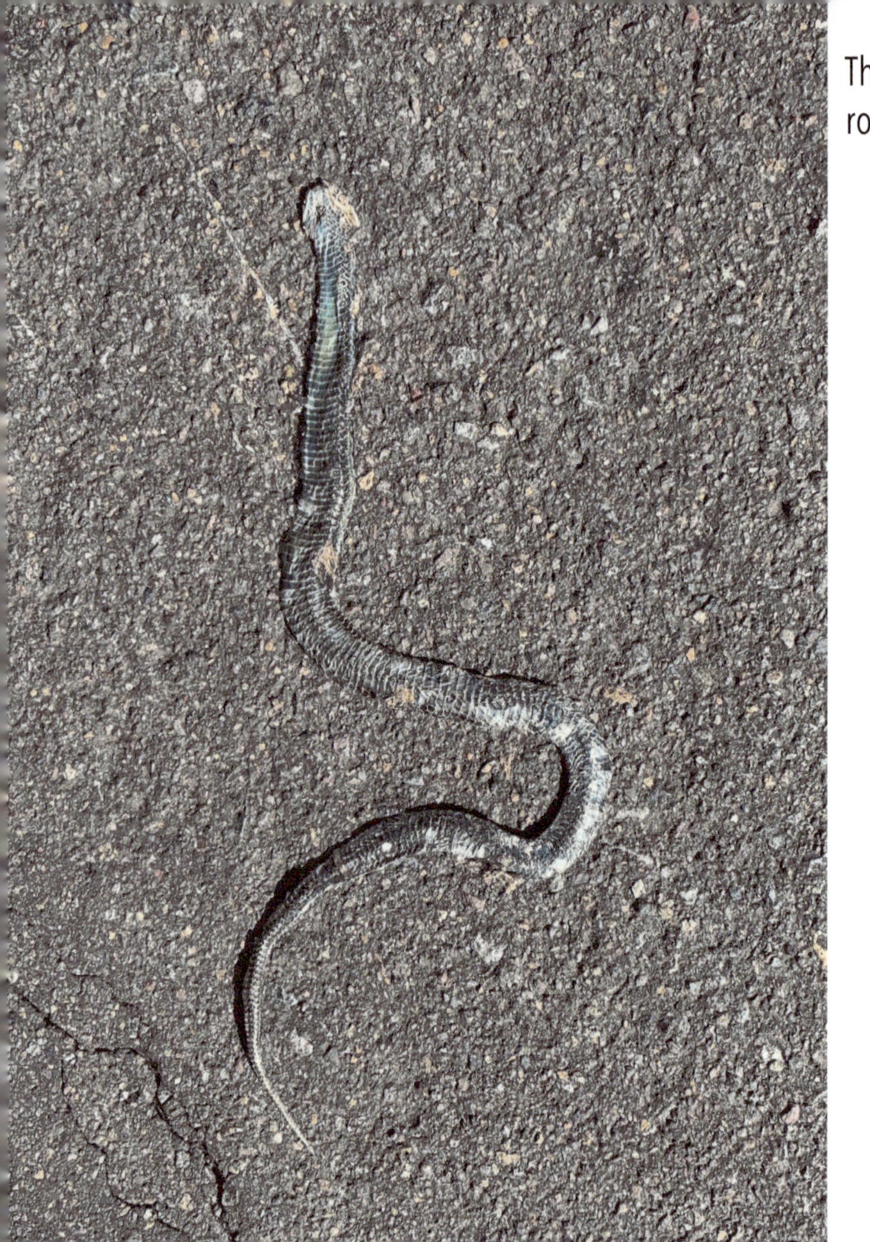

The end of the
road trip - 2019

Construction
roadkill - 2019

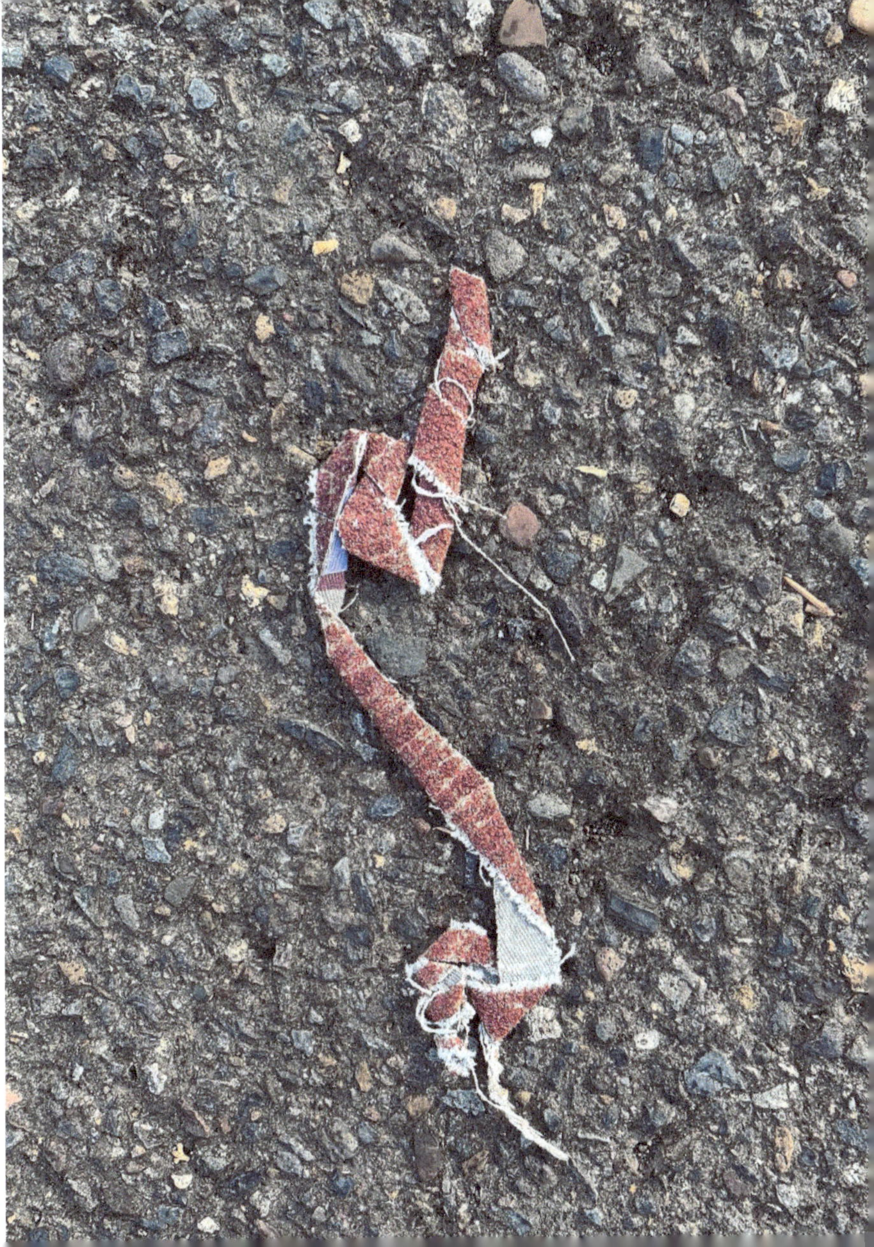

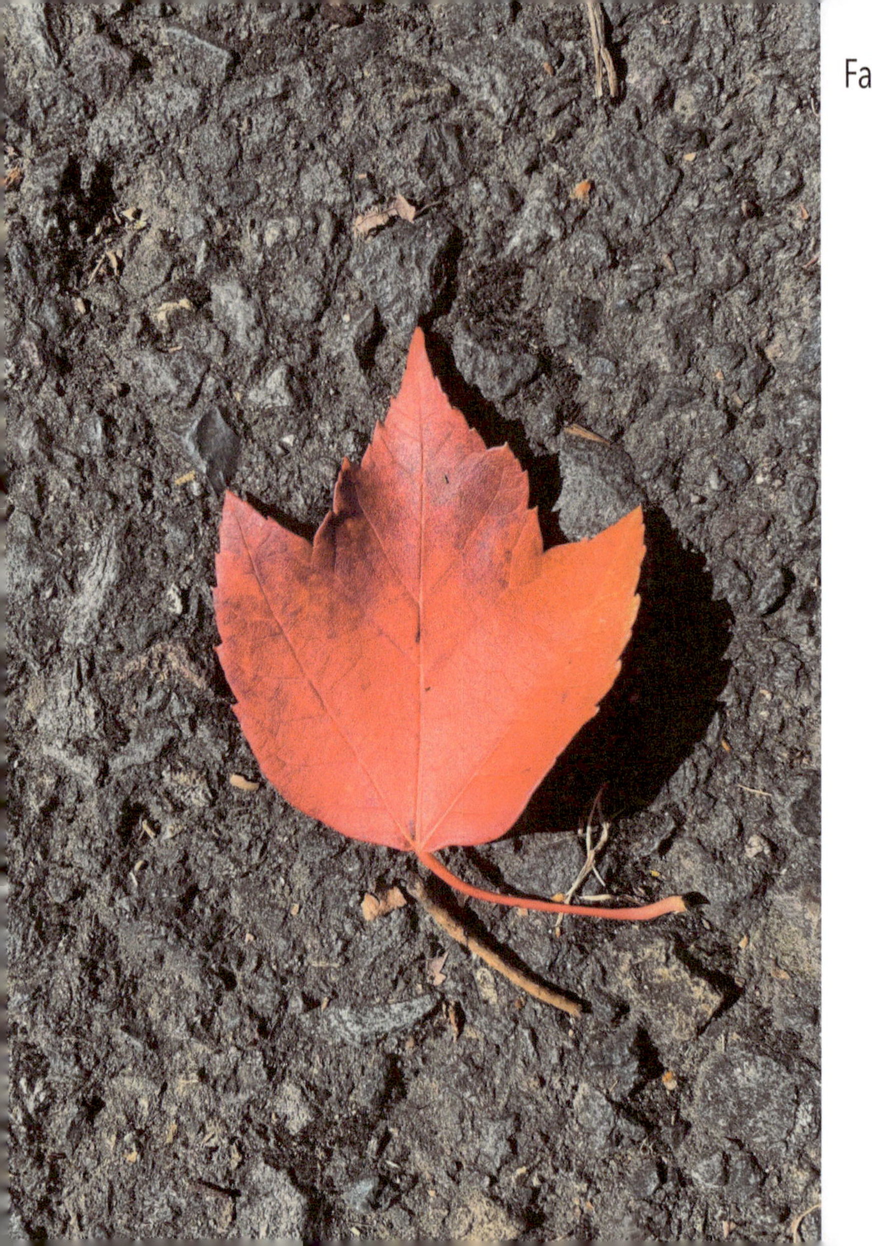

Fall - 2019

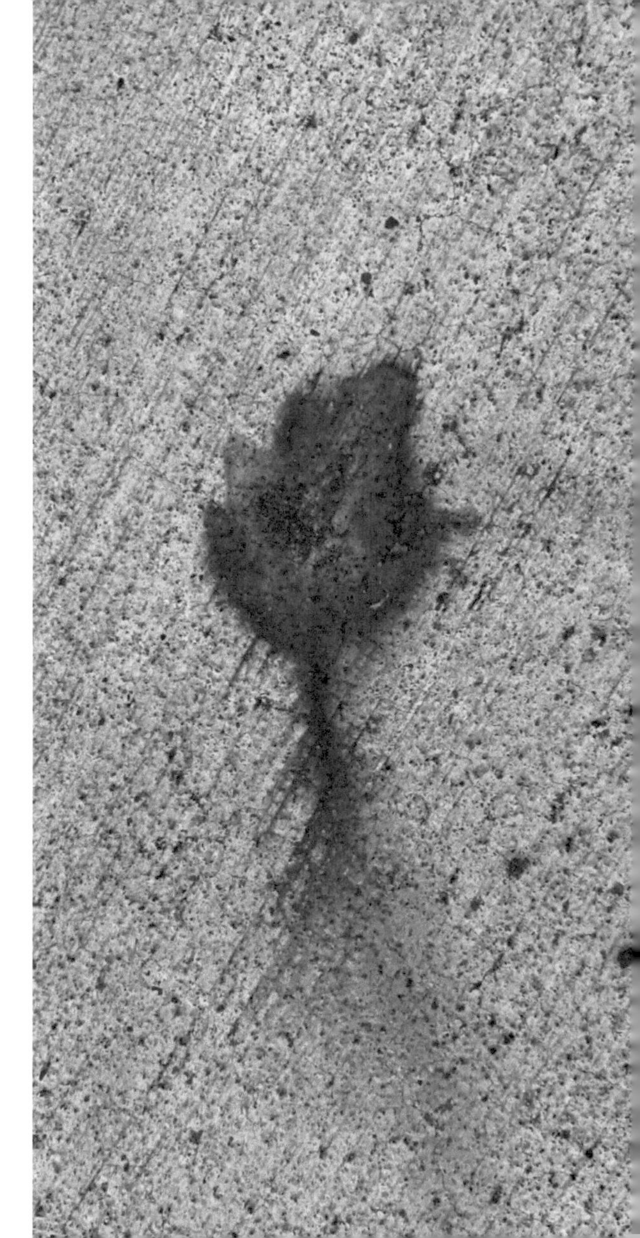

Fall + water + time - 2019

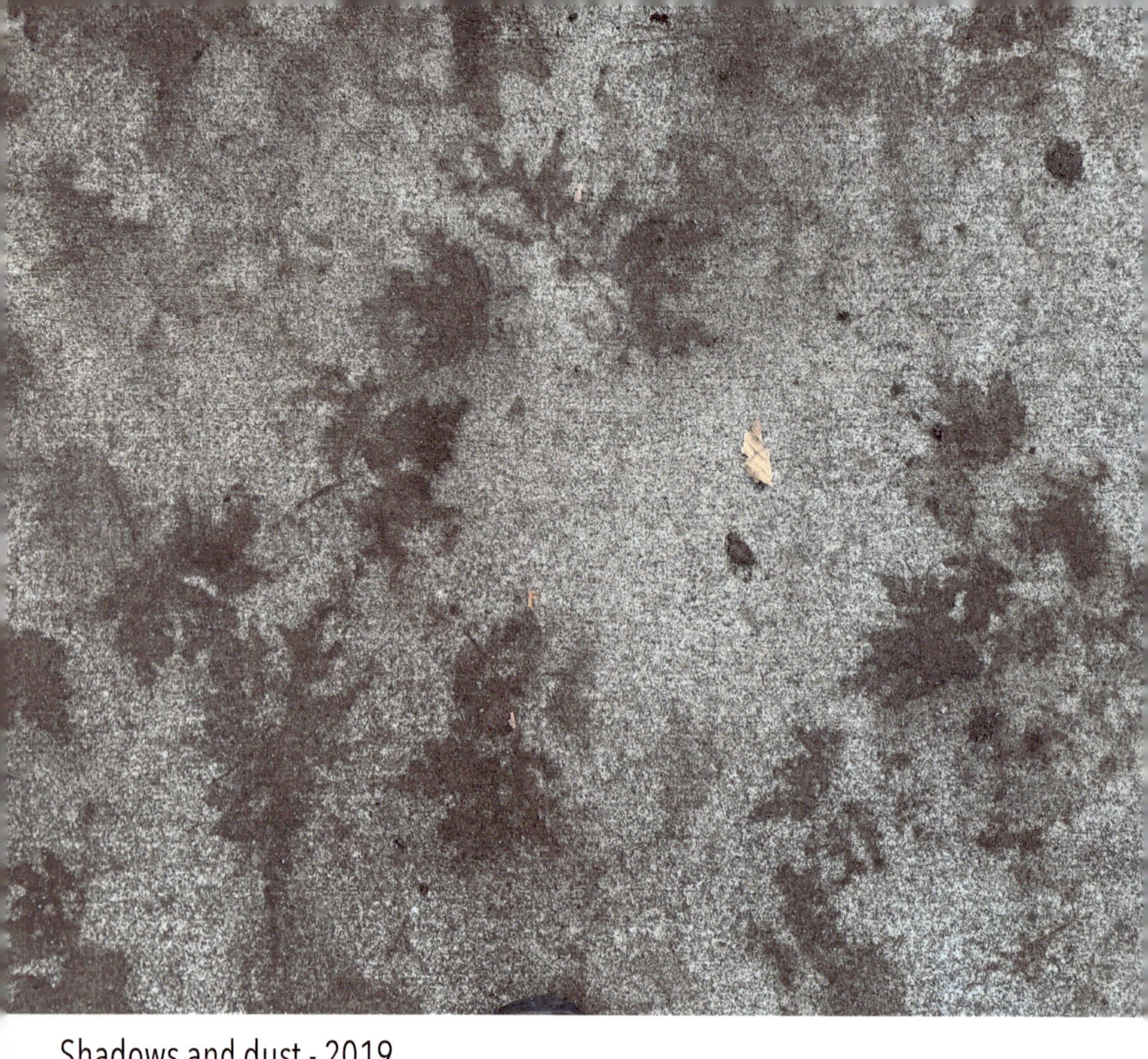

Shadows and dust - 2019

Shadow - 2019

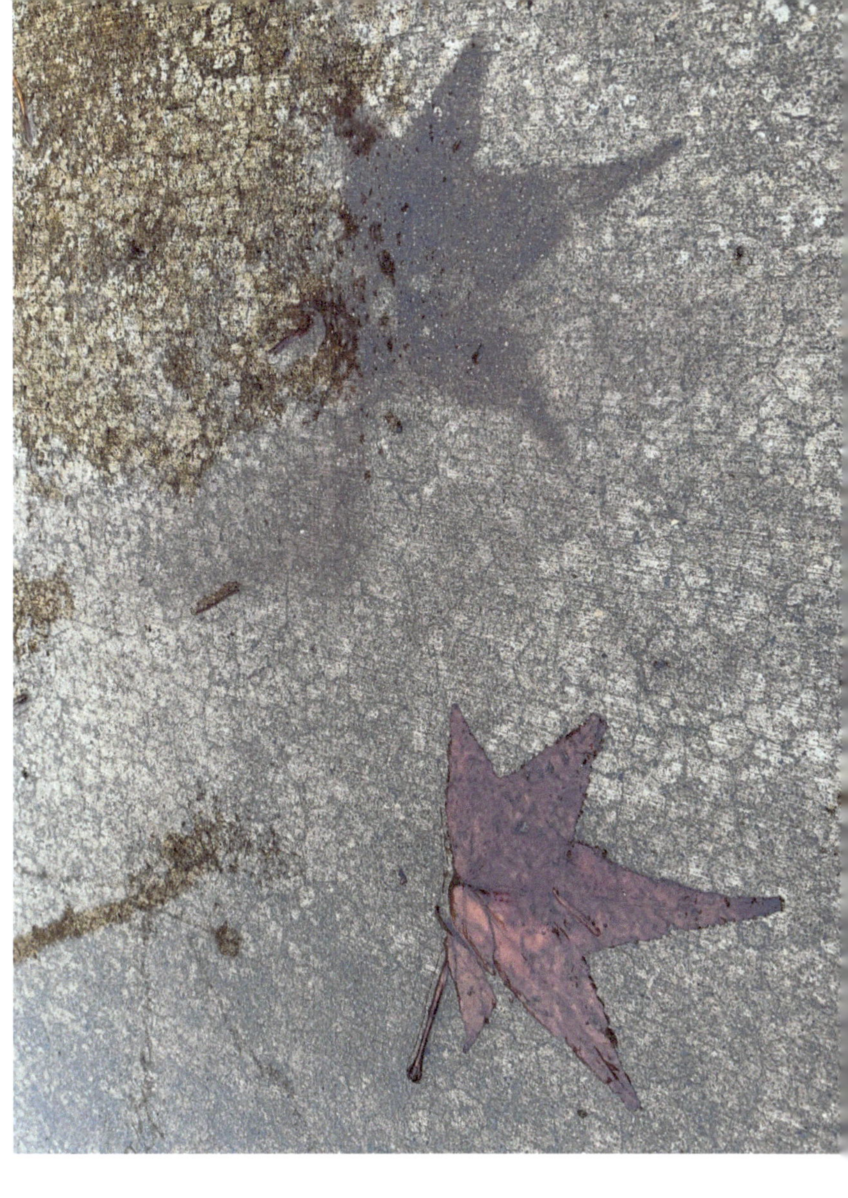

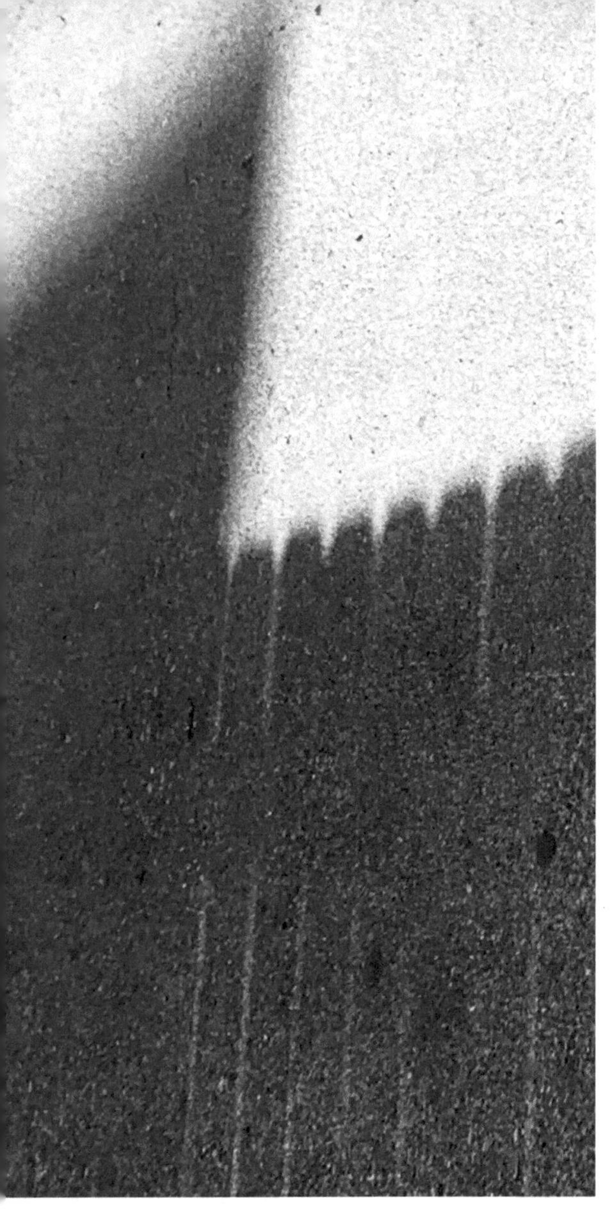

Skyline - 2019

Sewer asterisk, make up your own joke - 2019

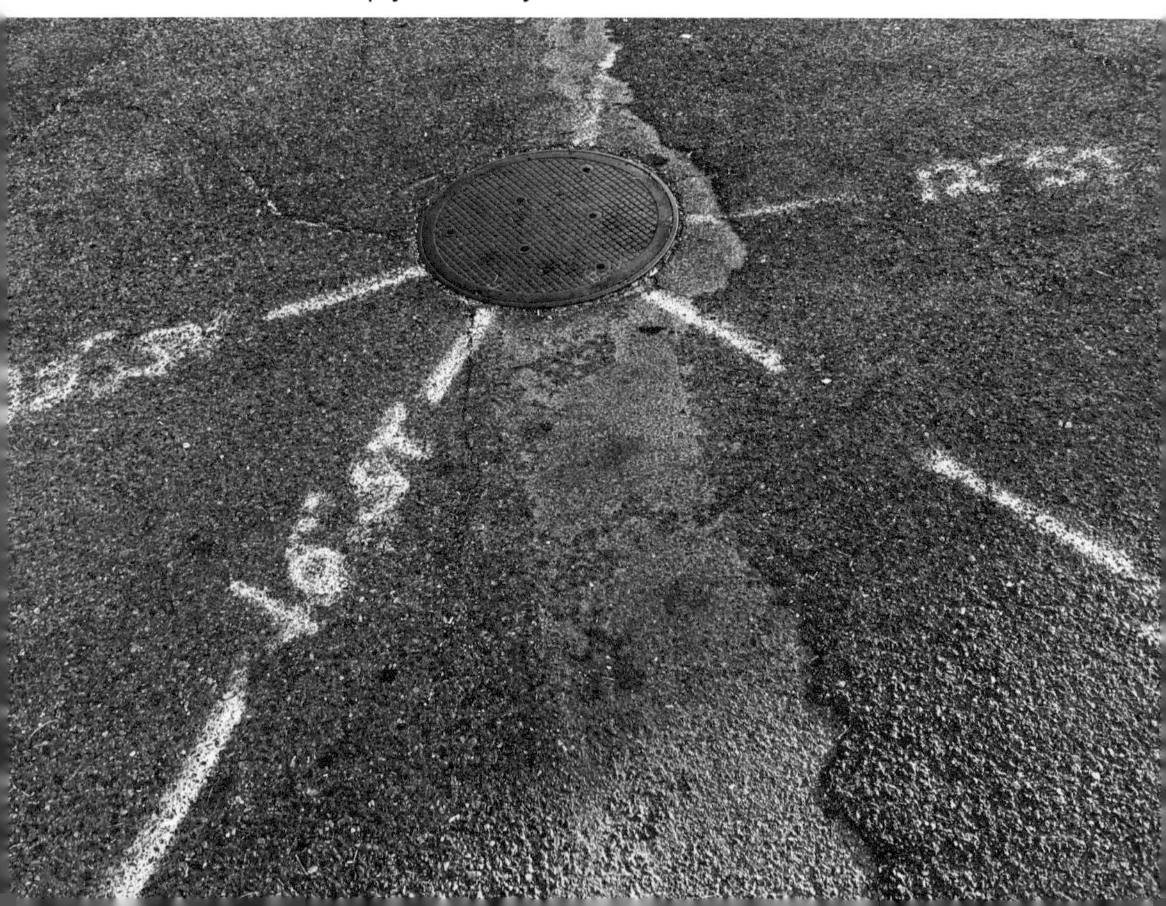

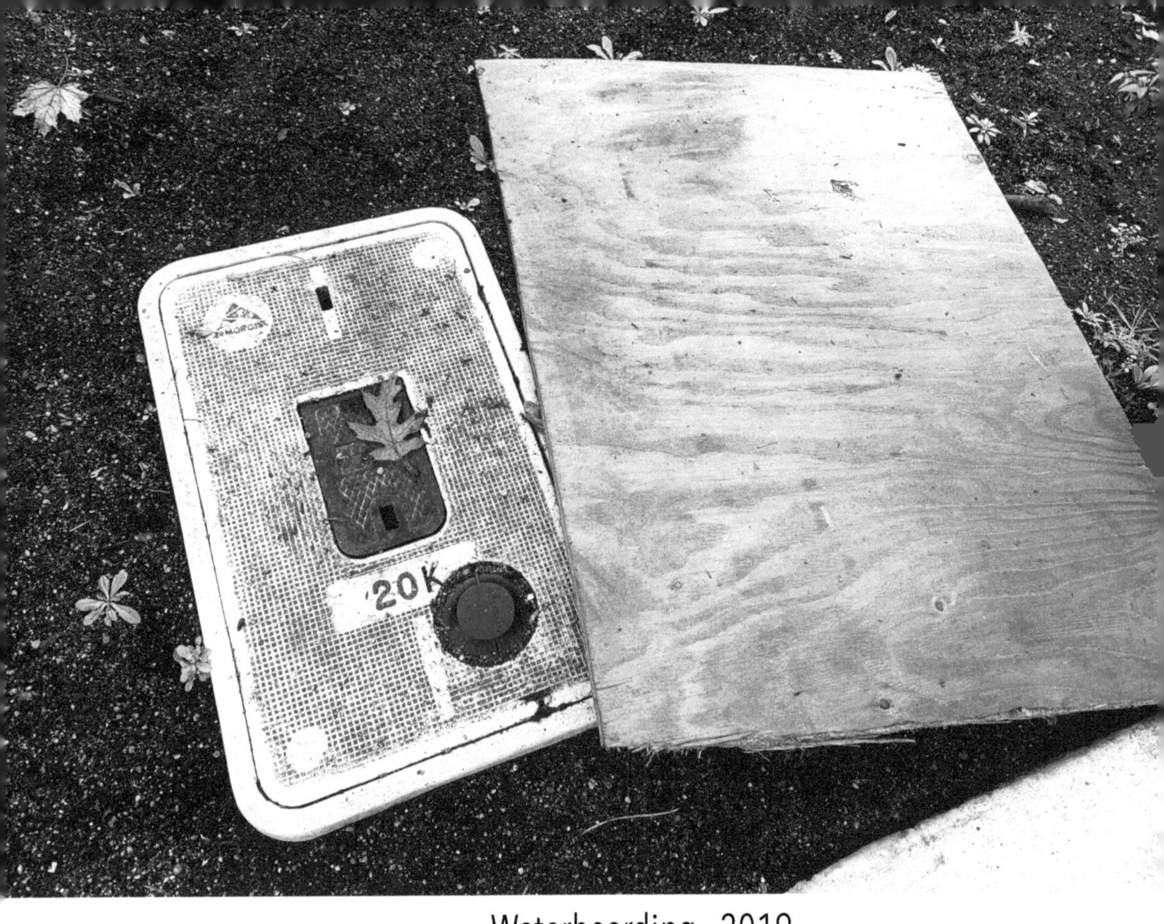

Waterboarding - 2019

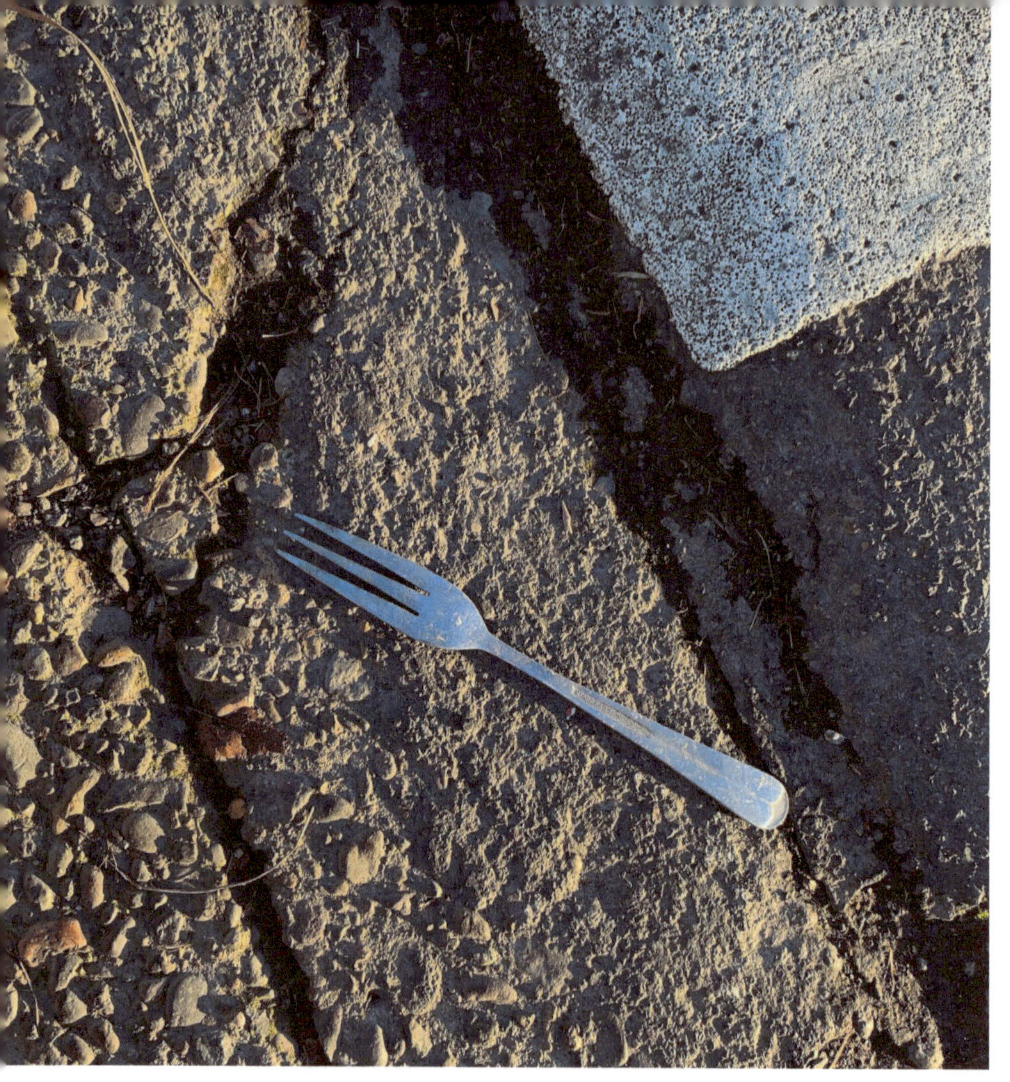

If you're going to take the fork in the road, please
use gloves - 2019

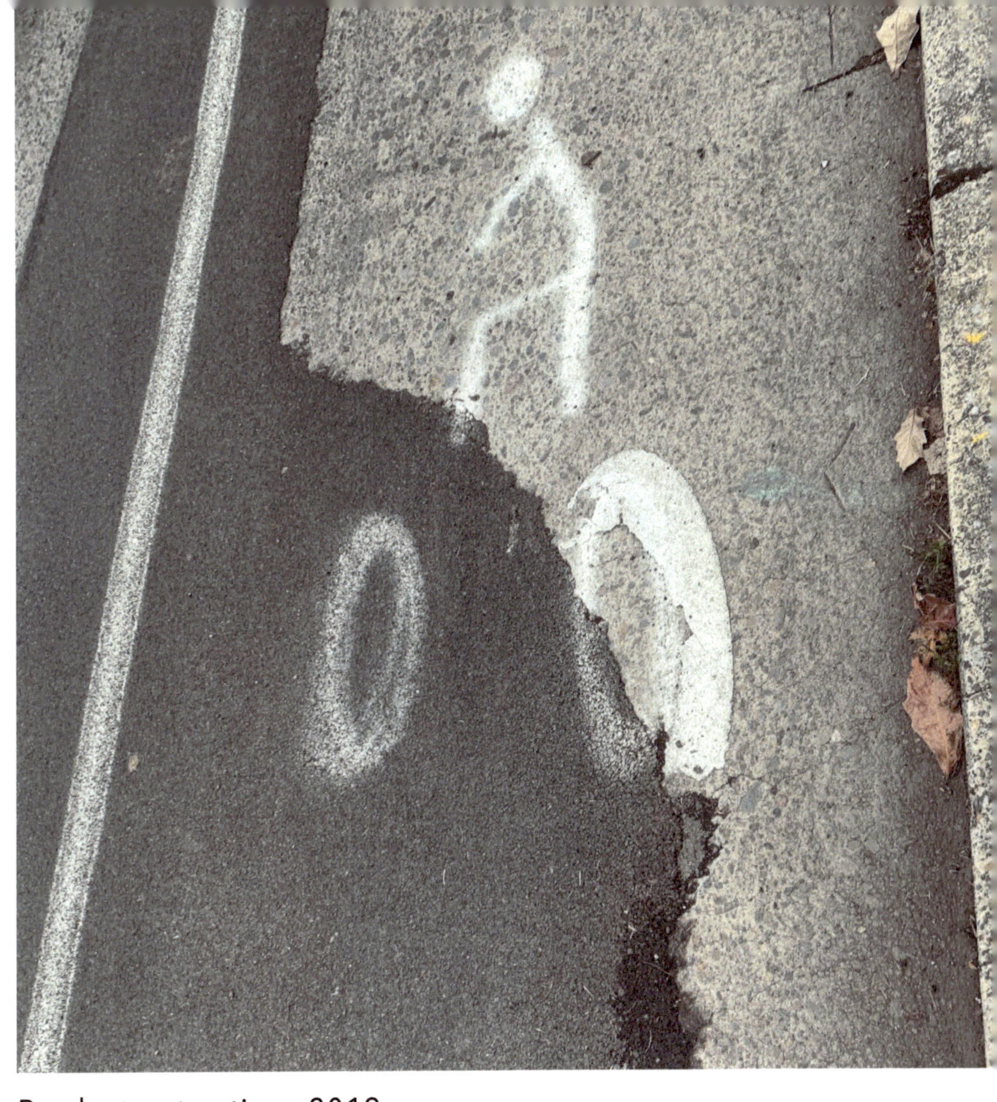

Road art restoration - 2019

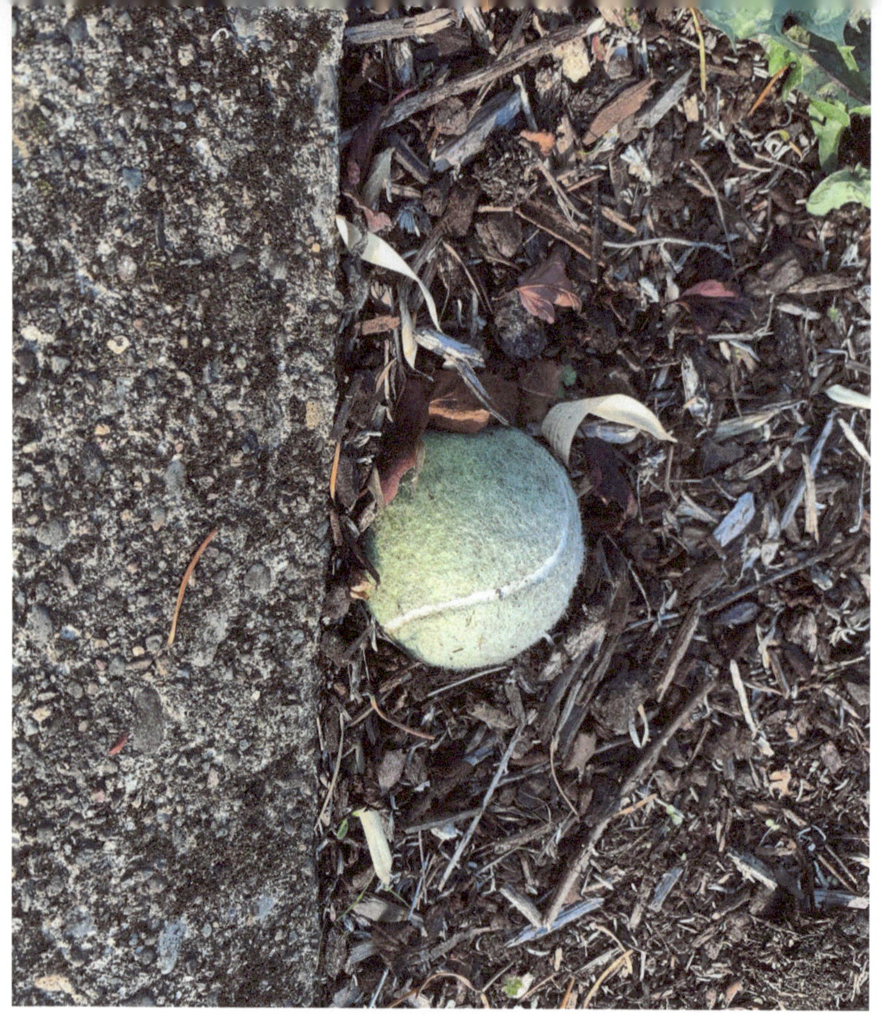

Ball - 2019

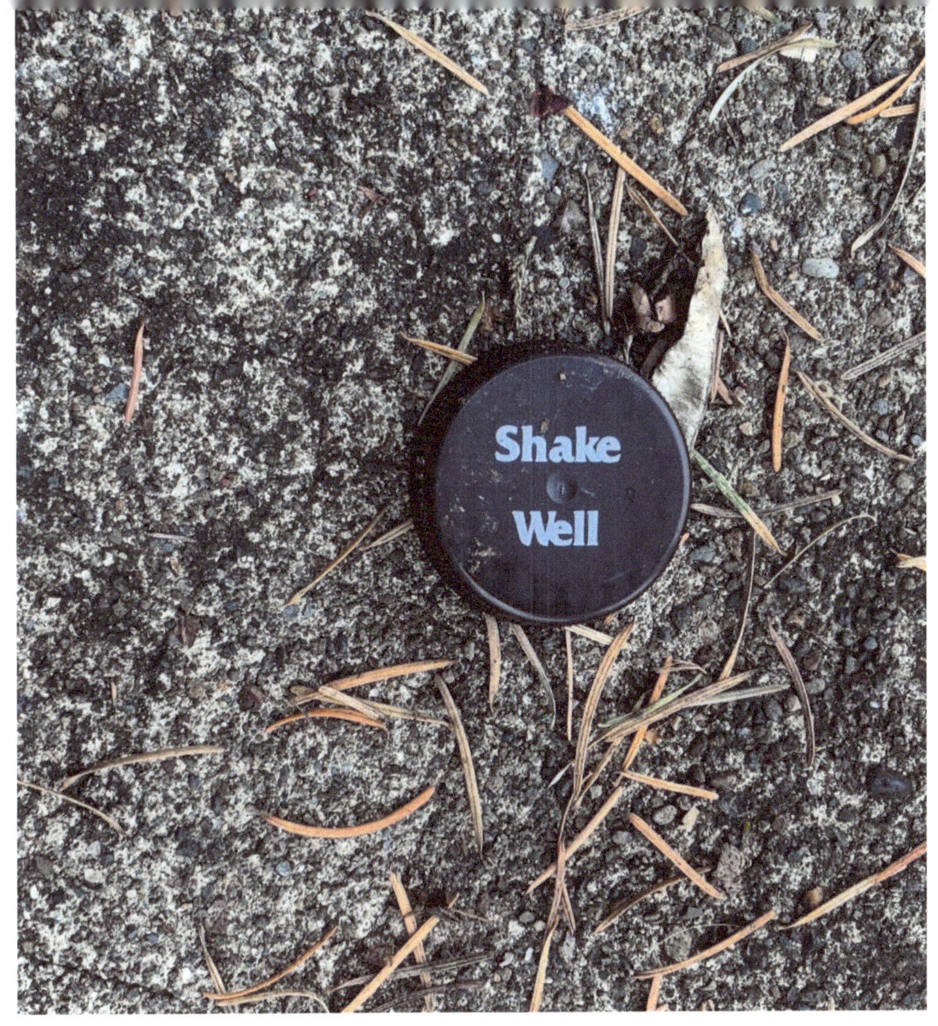

2.5 magnitude or less, please - 2019

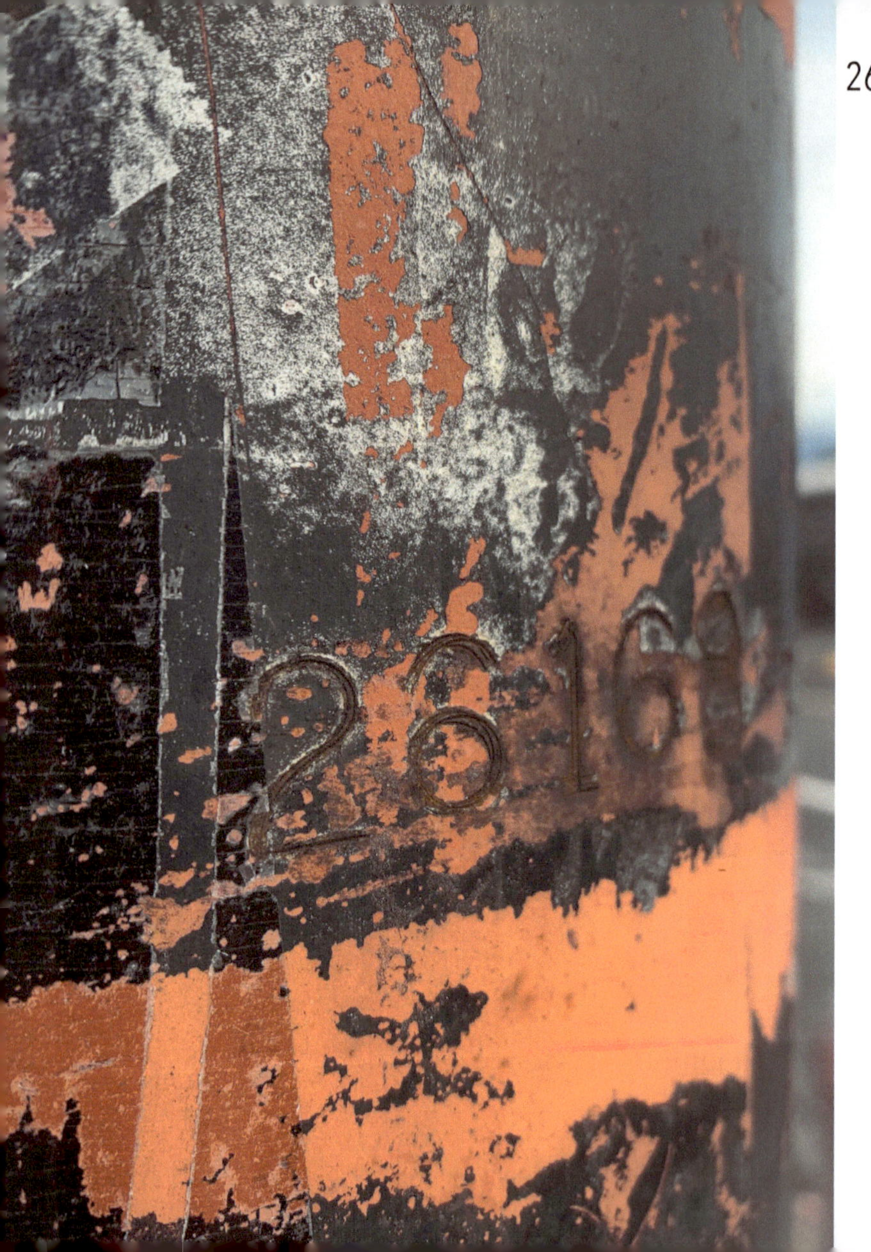

26168 - 2019

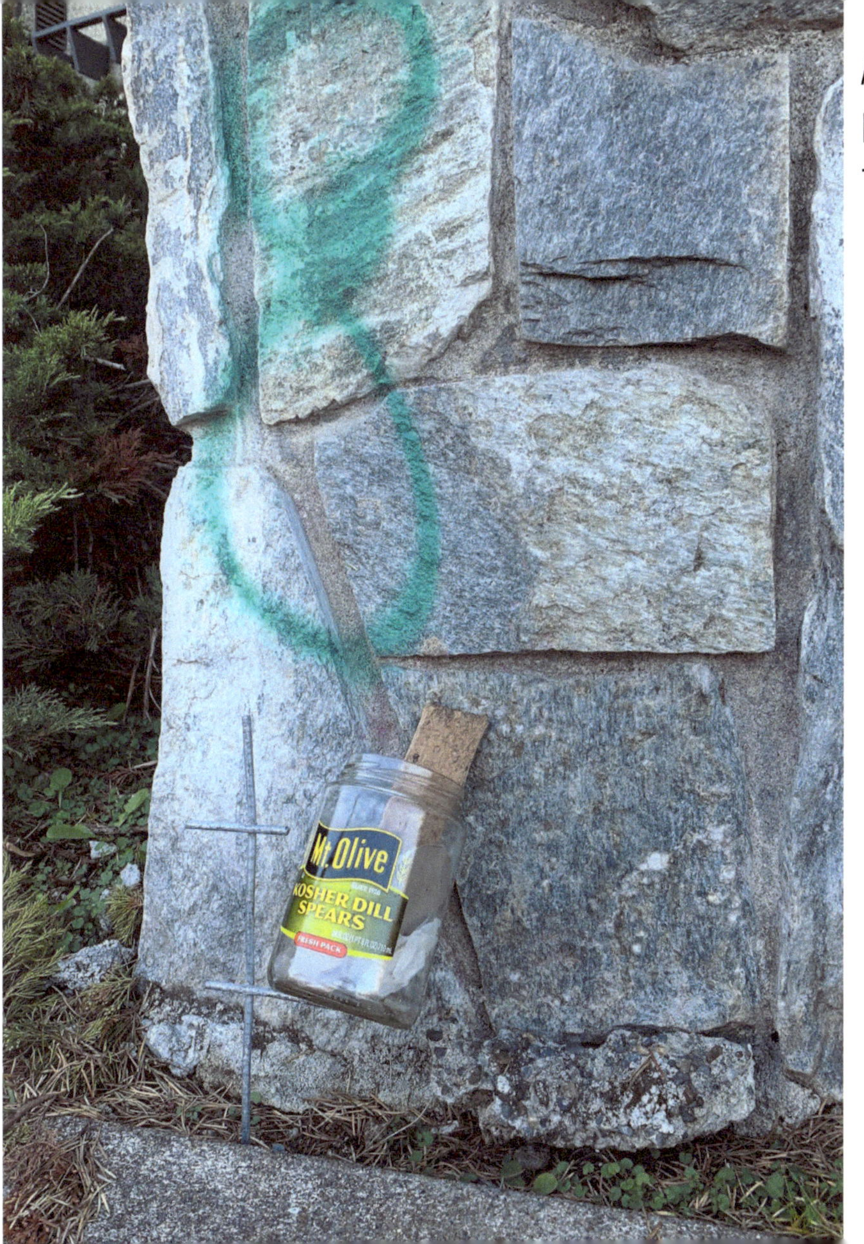

Alter to the
pickle god(s)?
- 2019

Norm - 2019

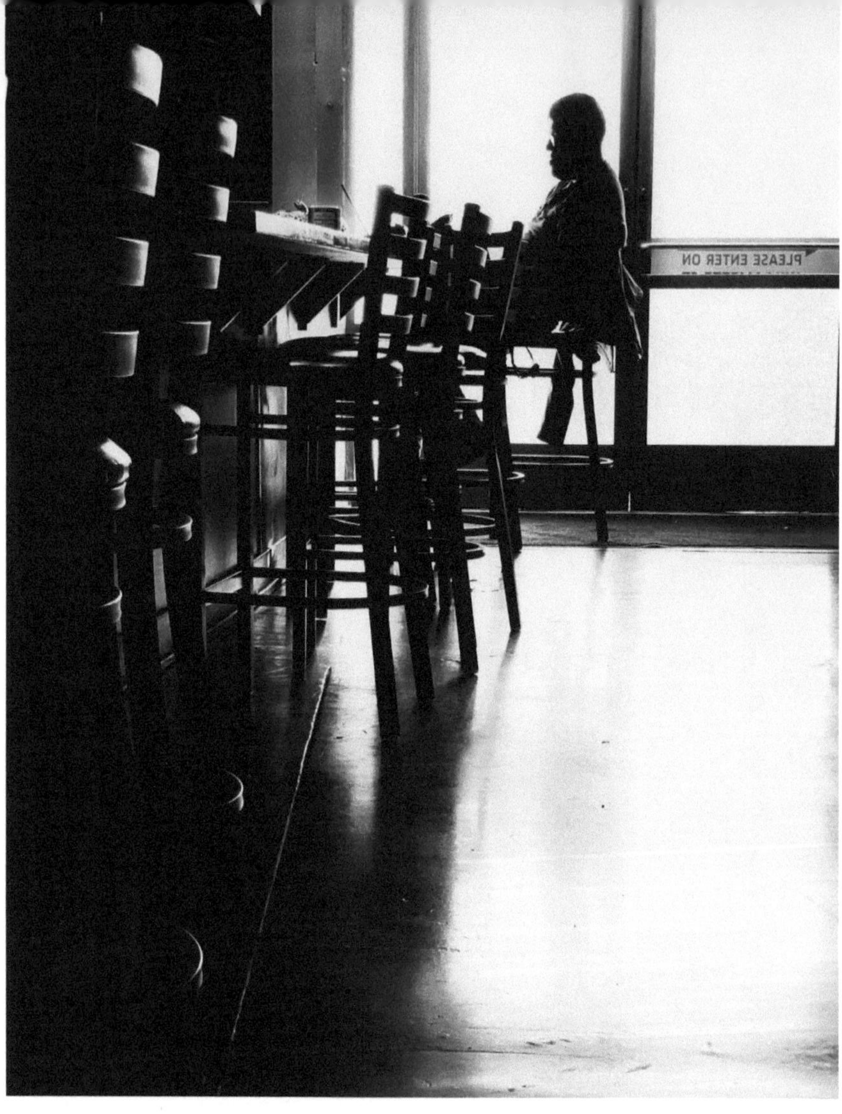

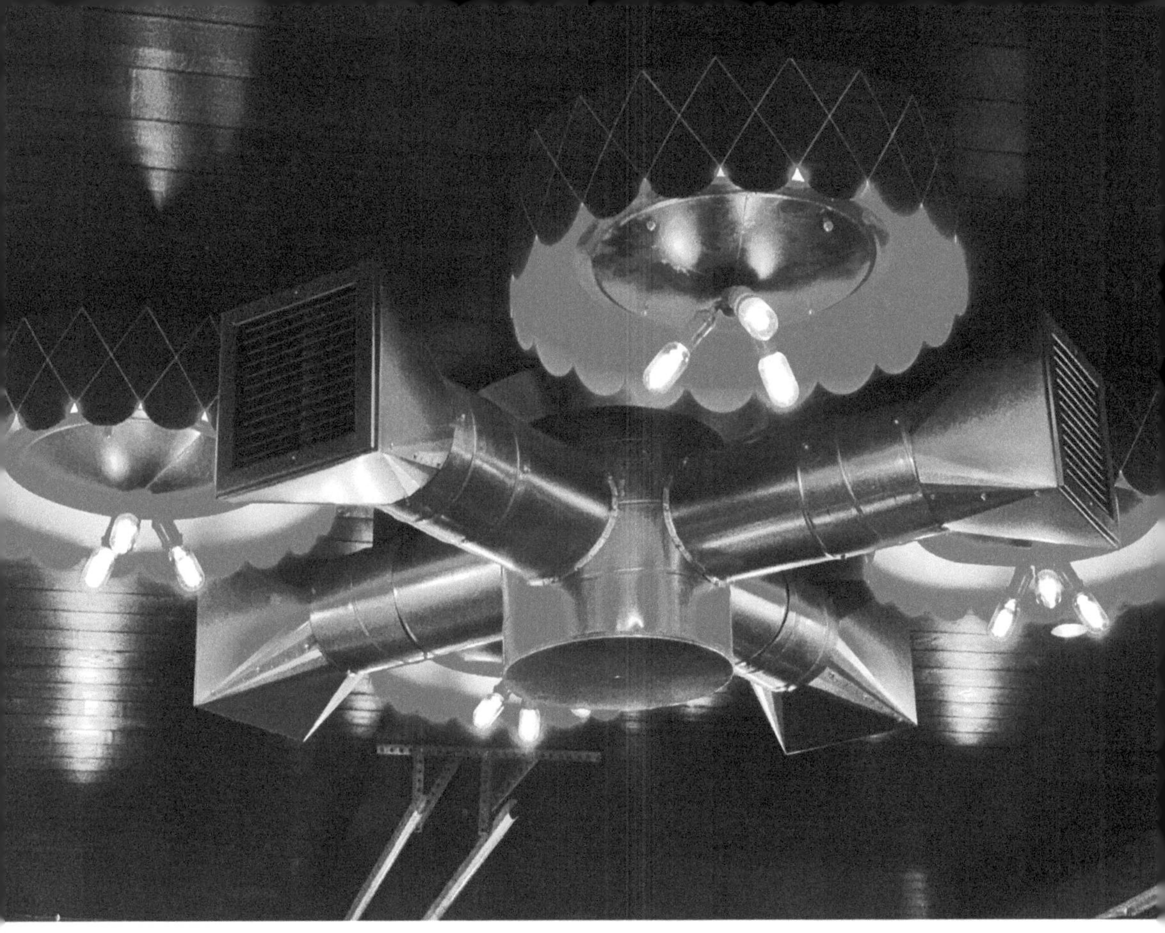

Spielberg HVAC - 2019

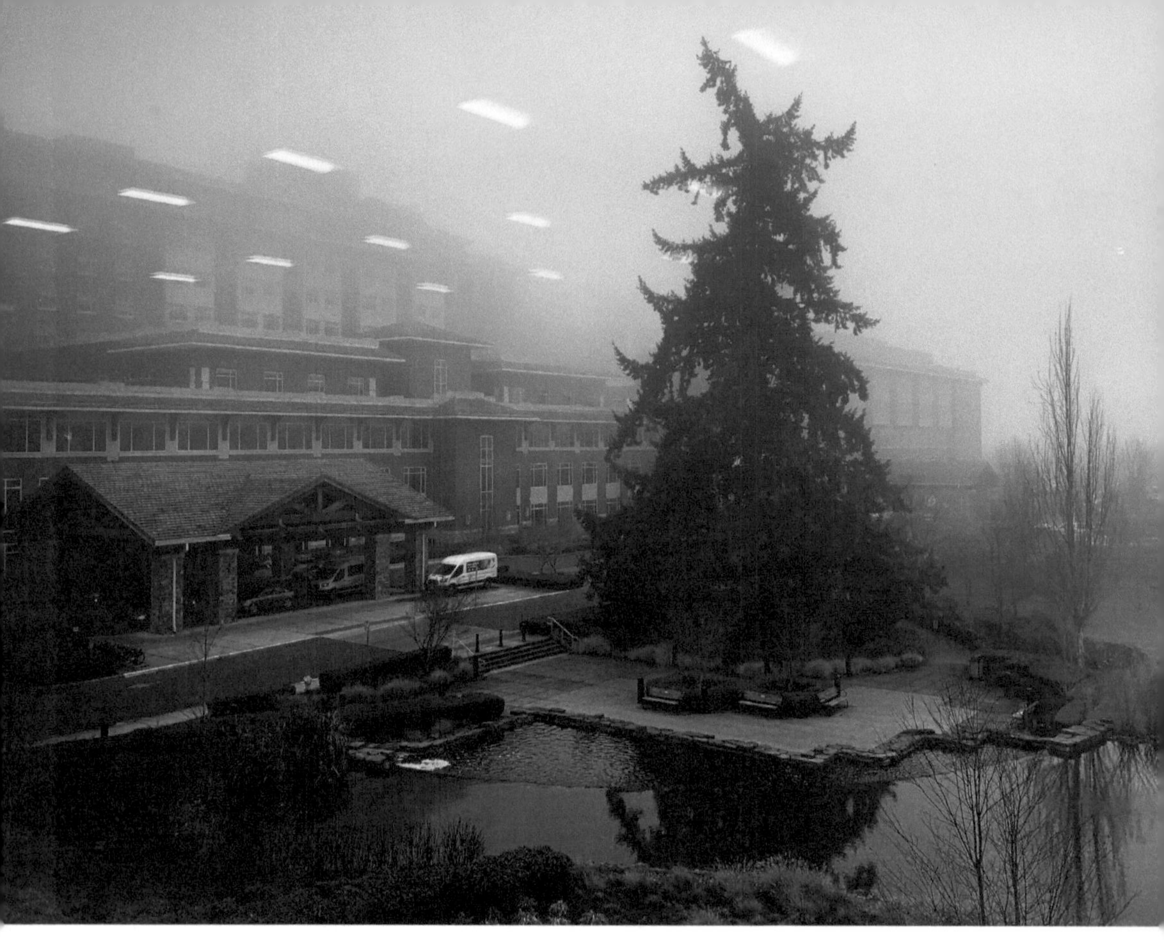

Waiting in the fog, from the inside - 2019

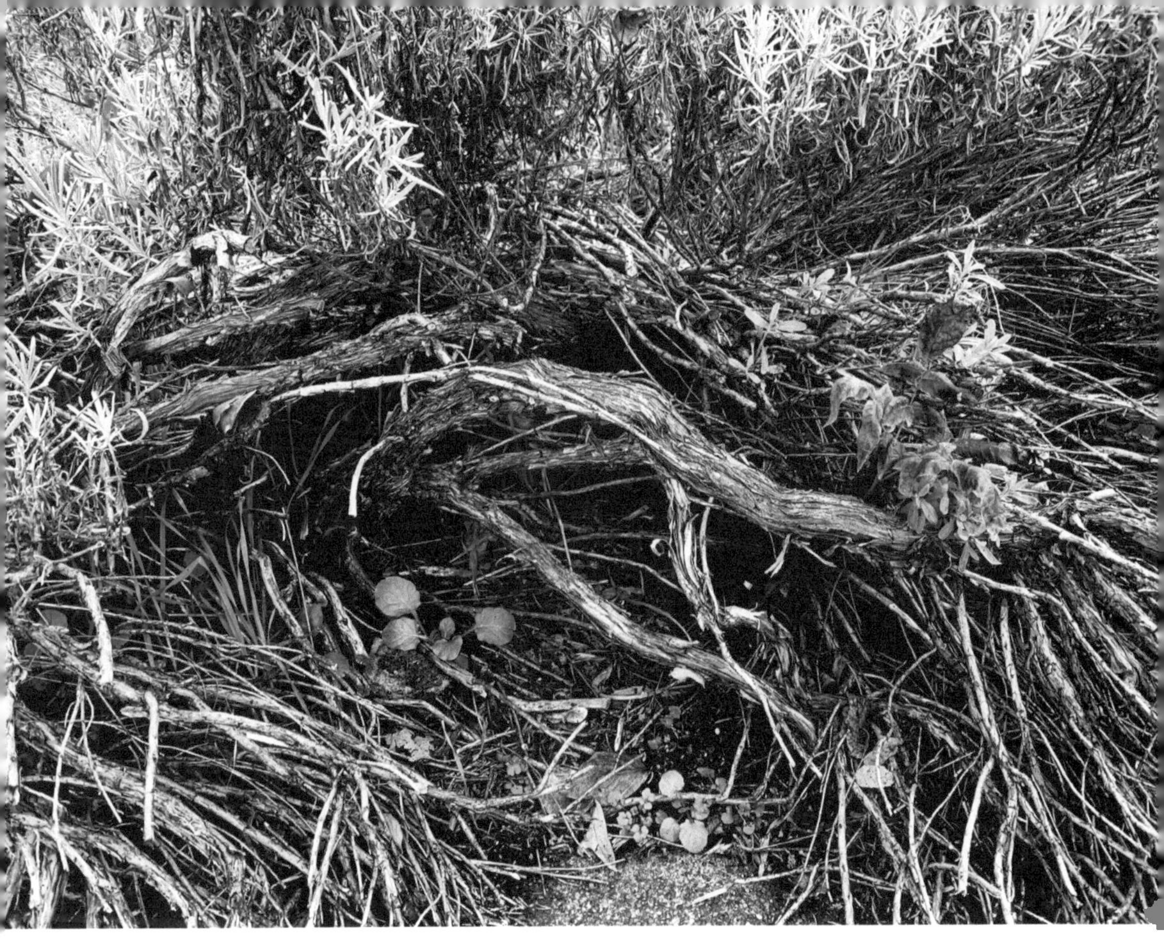

Old lavender - 2019

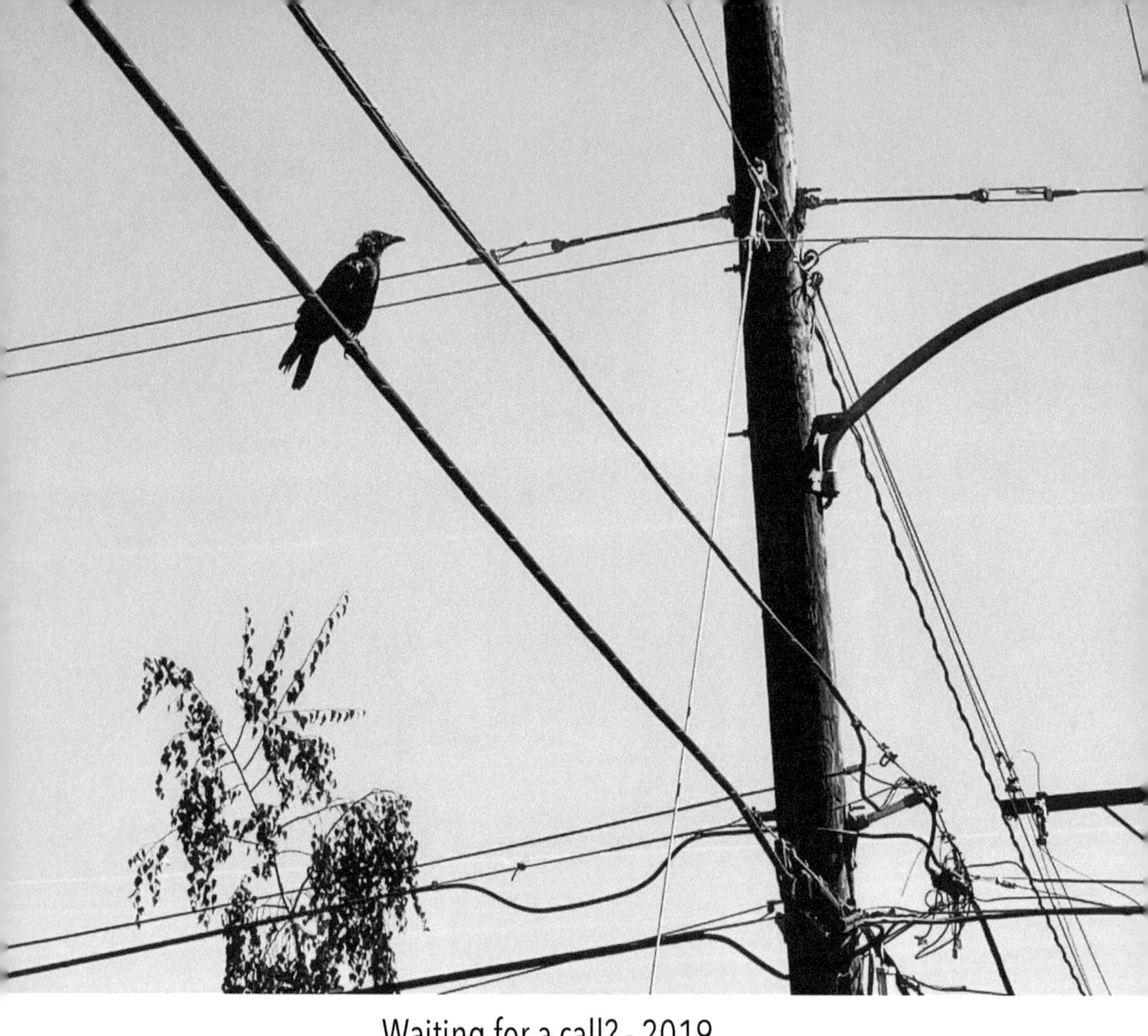

Waiting for a call? - 2019

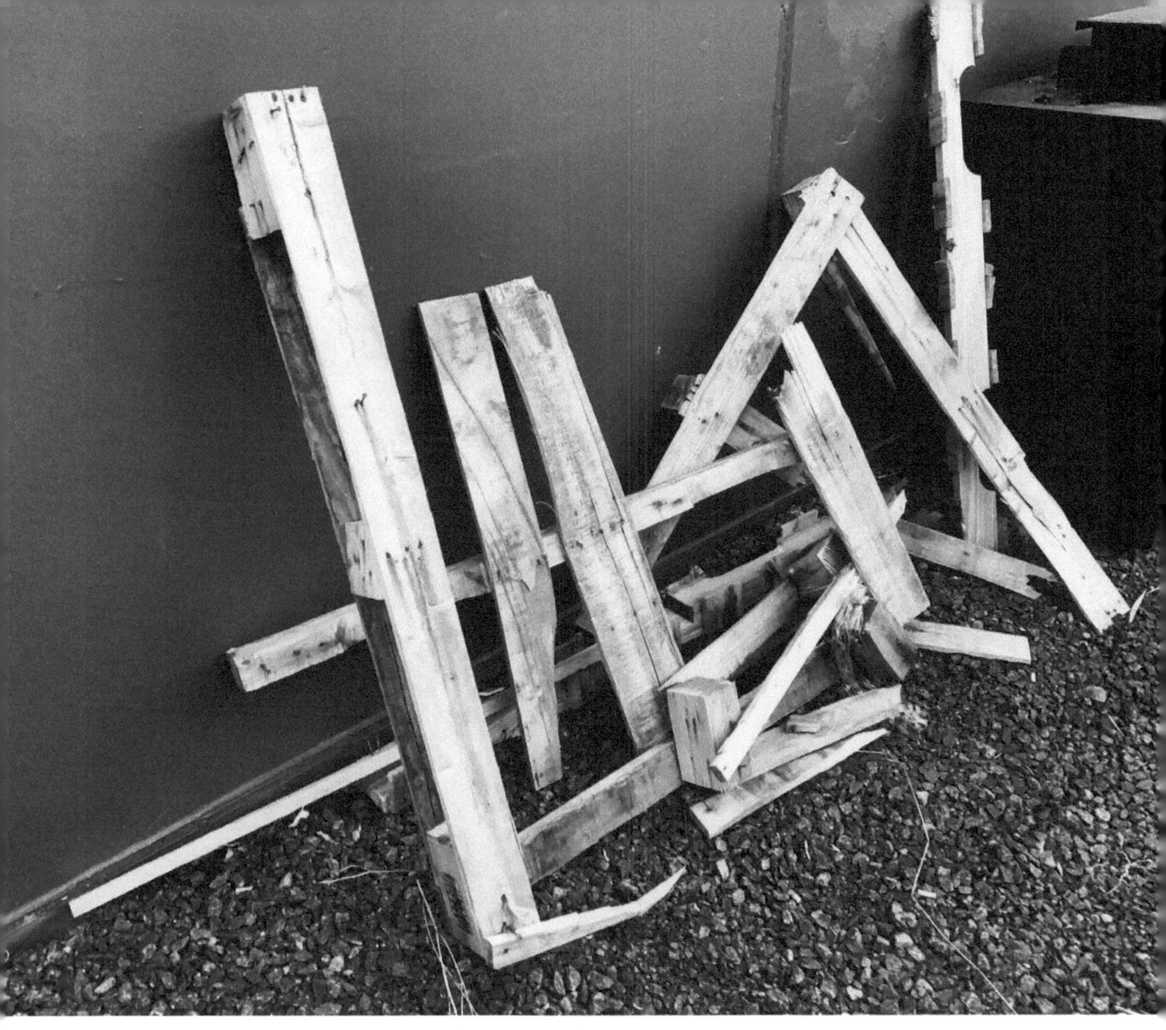

His palate was destroyed - 2019

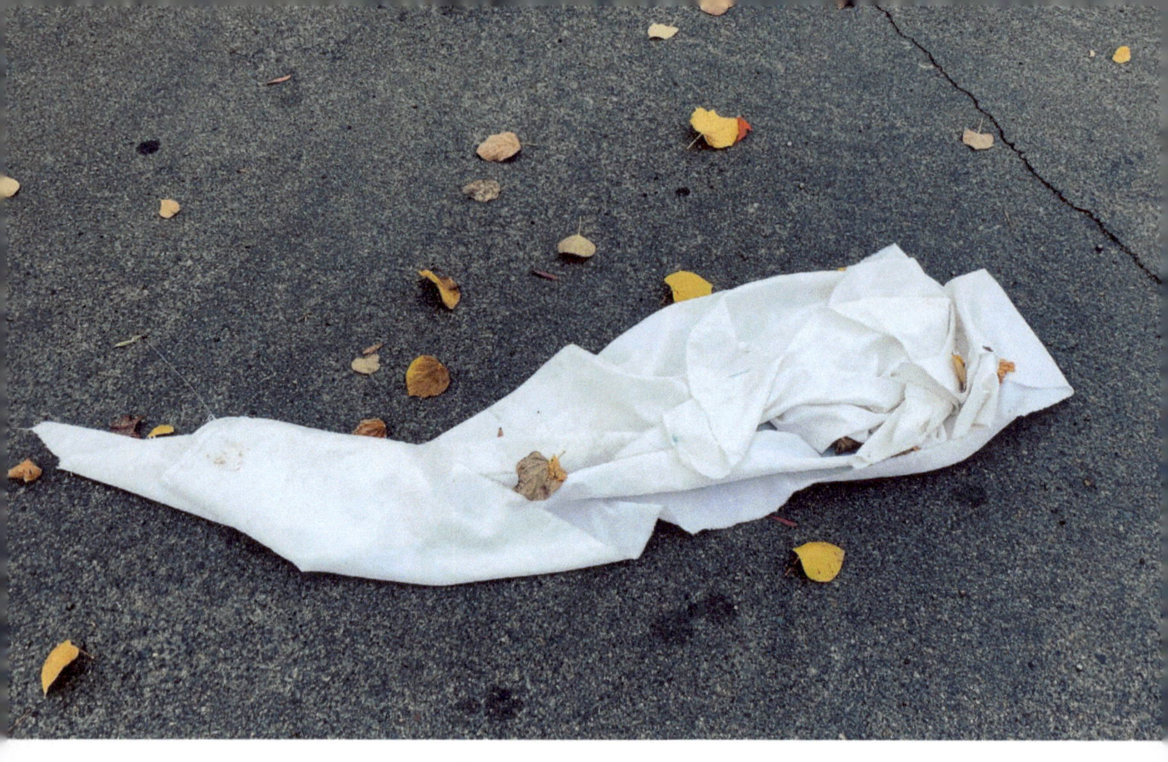

Don't lose your sheet man - 2019

I hope you enjoyed the photos.
Proceeds from the sale of this book will go toward
the funding of the Tiny Art Gallery project.

TinyArtGallery.org for more information.